The End of Philosophy

Martin Heidegger

Works

Coeditors J. Glenn Gray
Colorado College

Joan Stambaugh
Hunter College of the City University of New York

By Martin Heidegger

Being and Time
Discourse on Thinking
Hegel's Concept of Experience
Identity and Difference
What Is Called Thinking?
On the Way to Language
Poetry, Language, Thought
On Time and Being
The End of Philosophy

The End of Philosophy

MARTIN HEIDEGGER

Translated by Joan Stambaugh

Harper & Row, Publishers
New York, Evanston, San Francisco, London

Originally published by Verlag Günther Neske, Pfullingen, as a part of Volume II of *Nietzsche*, copyright 1961 by Verlag Günther Neske, Pfullingen. "Overcoming Metaphysics" is taken from *Vorträge und Aufsätze*, copyright 1954 by Günther Neske, Pfullingen. English translation by Joan Stambaugh.

FIRST EDITION

Designed by Ann Scrimgeour

Library of Congress Cataloging in Publication Data

Heidigger, Martin, 1889–
    The end of philosophy.

    (His Works)
    Contains 4 chapters, the first 3 being from the
end of vol. 2 of Heidegger's Nietzsche and the last
from his Vorträge und Aufsätze.
    CONTENTS: Stambaugh, J. Introduction.—Metaphysics
as history of being.—Sketches for a history of being as metaphysics. [etc.]
    1. Metaphysics. 2. Ontology. I. Title
B3279.H47E55   110   73–16214
ISBN 0–06–063856–7

CONTENTS

INTRODUCTION
By Joan Stambaugh

This small, highly condensed volume contains Heidegger's most explicit attempt to show the history of Being as metaphysics. Chapter four, "Overcoming Metaphysics," is taken from the German volume, *Vorträge und Aufsätze*. The other three chapters, "Metaphysics as History of Being," "Sketches for a History of Being as Metaphysics," and "Recollection in Metaphysics," are taken from the end of Volume II of *Nietzsche*. The remainder of *Nietzsche* will be published in two volumes, one volume containing the material on nihilism and a final volume containing the material on Nietzsche proper. This present book contains little on Nietzsche as such; but, rather, it represents the fruit of the two German volumes entitled *Nietzsche*. It is published first because it contains Heidegger's most comprehensive treatment of the history of Being as metaphysics, beginning with Plato and Aristotle and continuing up through Schelling and Kierkegaard.

At the beginning of *Being and Time*, Heidegger states that he wishes to accomplish two things: (1) an interpretation of *Dasein* in terms of temporality and the explication of time as the transcendental horizon for the question of Being; and (2) a phenomenological destruction of the history of ontology. One might say that this present volume comes as close as anything Heidegger has published to carrying out such a "destruction." But apart from the fact that the somewhat misleading and ambiguous term "destruction" has been subject to inappropriate criticism, and therefore needs to be clarified, the intention in this book by no means simply coincides with that expressed in *Being and Time*.

The original plan for *Being and Time*[1] consisted of two parts. Part one had three divisions, two of which were published in that volume: (1) the preparatory fundamental analysis of *Dasein;* (2) *Dasein* and temporality; and, finally, (3) Time and Being, which Heidegger later carried out in the form of a lecture.[2] Part two, which was to accomplish the phenomenological destruction of the history of ontology with the problematic of temporality as a guide, likewise had three divisions: (1) Kant's doctrine of schematism and time; (2) the ontological foundation of Descartes' *cogito sum;* and (3) Aristotle's essay on time. Of the three thinkers named, it is only to Kant that Heidegger has devoted several publications. Aristotle is discussed in a few essays and lectures; Descartes is a central figure throughout, but not the subject of a separate publication. In other words, of the originally planned six divisions of *Being and Time*, two are contained in that volume, two are more or less carried out in later separate publications, and the last two are mostly absorbed throughout Heidegger's writings.

Thus one might say that in his published works Heidegger has executed the first part of his philosophical enterprise, the interpretation of *Dasein* in terms of temporality and the explication of time as the transcendental horizon for the question of Being, in the form he originally envisaged for it. The second part, the "destruction," is carried out from a quite different philosophical foundation from that originally planned. I shall try to explain how the second foundation differs from the first, and then try to clarify the significance of that new foundation for the relations of: (1) Being-beings (the ontological difference); and (2) essence-existence (the "difference" or distinction of metaphysics). This is an interpretation in which I am partially aided and guided by Heidegger's answers to questions on

1. Cf. *Being and Time*, trans. by John Macquarrie and Edward Robinson (New York: Harper & Row, 1962), pp. 63–64.
2. Cf. *On Time and Being*, trans. by Joan Stambaugh (New York: Harper & Row, 1972).

the subject. It is also an interpretation which must of necessity remain an incomplete attempt.

The originally planned "destruction" was to be phenomenological in terms of a transcendental hermeneutic. These elements—phenomenology, hermeneutics, and transcendental philosophy—Heidegger linked indissolubly together in *Being and Time*, and it is precisely all three which he wishes to relinquish in his later thinking. Thus the destruction to be carried out can no longer have the character of these three elements, because they themselves constitute the history of ontology and are thus by no means capable of "destroying" or undoing that history. A destruction of the history of ontology must be undertaken in terms of the history of Being[3] and must be thought from the Appropriation. It must lay bare the relation of the epochal transformations of Being to the Appropriation. Here, as well as in *Being and Time*, the term "destruction" means the unbuilding (*de-struere*) of the layers covering up the original nature of Being, the layers which metaphysical thinking has con-structed.

In his attempt to relinquish the emphasis which metaphysical thinking has placed on causality (Being thought *exclusively* as the *ground* of being), Heidegger, particularly in his later thinking, comes more and more to center on the relation of identity and difference. In this relation it is fundamentally *difference* which receives prime emphasis, since identity is not thought traditionally as a static, abstract equation, but as *belonging-together*, which makes sense only in terms of what *differs*. For Heidegger, to differ is literally to dif-fer, to per-dure, to carry, hold, and bear out the relation of what belongs together.

Heidegger's first formulation of this relation in *Being and Time* is the ontological difference, the difference between Being and beings. This ontological difference, named but not carried out in *Being and Time*, was never thought by metaphysics and would have to be

3. Cf. p. 1.

experienced in a new way outside of metaphysics. Thus the ontological difference remains for Heidegger something inaccessible in principle to metaphysics, something to be experienced and transformed in terms of Appropriation.

What does metaphysics, which Heidegger defines as the separation of essence and existence that began with Plato, have to do with the ontological difference of Being and beings? One might say that the tradition, particularly the medieval tradition, would equate these two distinctions. Being (*esse*) is the essence of beings, of what exists (*existentia*), the essence in the sense of the universal One which unifies everything. For Heidegger, the distinction essence-existence actually belongs in the tradition on the side of Being, but the *difference* between Being and beings, although constantly presupposed by all metaphysics, was never thought. Only when metaphysics reaches its completion does the possibility arise of transforming the ontological difference, of thinking it from the unthought presupposition of all metaphysics back to its essential origin in Appropriation.

The greater part of this volume is engaged in working out what happened in the history of Being as metaphysics. With Plato's distinction of essence (whatness) and existence (thatness), the difference between Being and beings is obscured, and Being as such is thought exclusively in terms of its relation to beings as their first cause (*causa prima, causa sui*) and thus itself as the highest of those beings (*summum ens*). Thus metaphysics as the history of Being, as the history of the epochal transformations of Being, is precisely the history of the *oblivion* of Being. When the distinction of essence and existence arises, it is essence, whatness, which takes priority. The priority of essence over existence leads to an emphasis on beings. The original meaning of existence as *physis*, originating, arising, presencing, is lost, and existence is thought only in contrast to essence as what "factually" exists. In contrast to what "factually" exists here and now, Being is set up as permanent presence, a presen*ce* (nominal) abstracted from presenc*ing* (verbal) in terms of time-space.

This volume traces the history of the epochal transformations of Being right up to Heidegger's own thinking in *Being and Time*, and points beyond that to what he has to say about the Appropriation. As he remarks, the essential nature of Being can be explained in terms of the Appropriation, but the Appropriation can in no way be understood as a form of "Being."

It is in the spirit of these remarks about metaphysics as the history of the oblivion of Being that the title of this volume is to be understood. The end of philosophy does not mean for Heidegger that philosophy as such has become a thing of the past, a pursuit which has outlived its meaningfulness for human nature. Nor does Heidegger mean that philosophy in its essential sense has fulfilled its *telos*, that the "hard labor of the concept" (Hegel) has accomplished its task. Rather, he means that philosophy as *metaphysics* has come to a completion which now offers the possibility of a more original way of thinking.

The following questions and answers, which circle around the relation of Being, time, and Appropriation, are appended in the hope that they might throw additional light on these problems.[4]

1. *Temporality.*

QUESTION: What happens to the concept of temporality, so central in *Being and Time*, in your later thinking? Is there a relationship between temporality and Appropriation?

ANSWER: Temporality is "central" in *Being and Time* because the question of Being as such in the sense of presence starts with an analytic of human being which keeps itself ecstatically open to Being.

As a consequence of the turn, temporality is not given up but becomes the question of time and Being. The "temporality" of the Appropriation which temporalizes is the four-dimensional nearness

---

4. These questions were answered by Heidegger in writing in the summer of 1970, after being formulated by the editors. They are here translated with his permission.

bringing presencing near. The Appropriation is without destiny *(geschicklos)* because it itself sends presence. It is, however, not time-less in the sense of nearness. It is neither "in time" nor is it the "temporality" of human being, but rather brings each in a different way into its own.

In "Time and Being," however, the relation of the Appropria-tion and the human being of mortals is consciously excluded.

2. *Ontological Difference.*

QUESTION: Does the ontological difference disappear in the Ap-propriation? How is the ontological difference related to the distinc-tions (a) Being and beings; (b) *essentia* and *existentia?* What is the meaning of the ontological difference in the following passage:[5] "Perduring the truth of Being, grounded upon the explicit ground-ing of the ontological difference, that is, the distinction between beings and Being (outside of all metaphysics and existential philoso-phy)."

ANSWER: In *Identity and Difference* a sentence reads: "For us, formulated in a preliminary fashion, the matter of thinking is the difference *as* difference."[6] As such, the difference is "identity" thought in terms of the Appropriation, that means, the relation which perdures perdurance.

In the distinction "Being and beings," the difference is always already represented without being thought, unthought with respect to the differentiation. In all epochs of metaphysics, the difference remains the unexplained pre-supposition. The difference remains without place and determination.

Here the distinction of *essentia-existentia* belongs on the side of Being in the unthought difference.

5. Cf. p. 70.
6. Cf. *Identity and Difference*, trans. by Joan Stambaugh (New York: Harper & Row, 1969), p. 47.

"The explicit grounding of the ontological difference" occurs in the "step back" from persisting in what is unthought to identity, but identity thought in the Appropriation.

The ontological difference disappears insofar as thinking *no* longer persists in its unthought element; the ontological difference does not disappear insofar as it is thought back to its essential origin (*Identity and Difference*, p. 65).

3. *Being.*

QUESTION: In contradistinction to the Being of beings, should Being itself be thought as the Appropriation? What is the relation between (a) thinking Being without regard to beings (that means not metaphysically as the highest being and the ground of beings, *causa sui*); and (b) "What do you make of the difference if Being as well as beings appear *by virtue of the difference*, each in its own way?" (*Identity and Difference*, pp. 63–64)?

ANSWER: "Being itself" means: The Appropriation can no longer be thought as "Being" in terms of presence.[7] "Appropriation" no longer names another manner and epoch of "Being." "Being" thought without regard to beings (i.e., always only in terms of, and with respect to, them) means at the same time: no longer thought as "Being" (presence).

If this happens, then the thinking thus transformed thinks the following: the ontological difference disappears in the Appropriation through the step back. It loses its decisiveness for thinking and is thus given up in a certain way in thinking.

A final question which was supposed to have "answered itself": Can anything more be said about the relation of (a) the epochal

7. *On the Way to Language*, trans. by Peter D. Hertz (New York: Harper & Row, 1971), p. 129n.

transformations of Being; (b) Appropriation; and (c) Expropriation
(kryptesthai)?

| The epochal transformations of Being | $\bigwedge$ Framing (Janus head) | Appropriation $\longleftrightarrow$ Expropriation |

Isn't Appropriation already in itself a double relation: (1) a "separable" relation in that through possibly overcoming Framing by the step back the epochal transformations of Being would be absorbed in Appropriation; and (2) an "inseparable" relation: Appropriation and Expropriation can never be separated from each other, but rather constitute a relation which is what is most original of all (but not original in the sense of being a cause)? Between the epochal transformations of Being and Appropriation reigns the relation of giving *(Es gibt)*, but not even this can be said of the relation Appropriation-Expropriation.

ONE

Metaphysics as History of Being
Whatness and Thatness in the Essential Beginning of Metaphysics: idea and energeia

One could take the following as a historical report about the history of the concept of Being.
Then what is essential would be missed.
But perhaps what is essential can at times hardly be said any other way.

"Being" means that beings are, and are not nonexistent. "Being" names this "That" as the decisiveness of the insurrection against nothingness. Such decisiveness emanating from Being at first arrives in beings, and here adequately, too. In these beings Being appears. So decisively has Being allotted beings to itself (in Being) that this does not need to be thought expressly. Beings give adequate information about Being.

"Beings" are considered what is actual. "Beings are actual." This sentence means two things. Firstly: The Being of beings lies in actuality. Then: As what is actual, Beings are "actual," that is, truly what-is. The actual is the completed act or product of an activity. This product is itself in turn active and capable of activity. The activity of what is actual can be limited to the capacity of producing a resistance which it can oppose to another actual thing in different ways. To the extent that beings act as what is actual,

Being shows itself as actuality. The true nature of Being has announced itself as "actuality" for a long time. "Actuality" often means "existence," too. Thus Kant speaks of the "proofs for God's existence." This is supposed to show that God is actual, that is, "exists." "The fight for existence" means the struggle of everything that lives (plant, animal, man) to become and remain actual. Metaphysics is acquainted with the question whether the real world, that is, the one "existing" now, is the best of all worlds or not. Being as the actuality of what is actual pronounces its most common metaphysical name in the word "existence" *(existentia)*. In the language of metaphysics, "actuality," "reality," and "existence" say the same thing. But what these names say is by no means unequivocal. This is not due to sloppiness of word usage, but comes rather from Being itself. It is easy for us and we like to appeal to the fact that everybody always knows what "Being," "actuality," "reality" and "existence" say. But in what way Being determines itself as actuality from acting and from work is obscure. Besides, "Being" would not be completely named in metaphysics if the saying of the Being of beings were satisfied with equating Being and existence.

Metaphysics has distinguished for ages between *what* beings are and *that* beings are, or are not. The scholastic language of metaphysics is acquainted with this distinction as that between essence and existence. *Essentia* means the *quidditas*, that which, for example, the tree as tree, as something growing, living, as tree*like*, is without any regard to the question whether and that this or that tree "exists." Here treelike is determined as *genos* in the double sense of origin and species, that is, as the *hen* to the *polla*. It is the One as the whence and as what is common to the many *(koinon)*. *Essentia* names that which something like an existing tree can be, if it exists; that which makes it possible as such a thing: possibility.

Being is divided into whatness and thatness. The history of Being as metaphysics begins with this distinction and its preparation. Metaphysics includes the distinction in the structure of the truth about beings as such as a whole. Thus the beginning of metaphysics is revealed as an event that consists in a determination of

Being, in the sense of the appearance of the division into whatness and thatness.

A support for the differentiating determination of *existentia* is now given by *essentia*. Actuality is distinguished from possibility. One could attempt to grasp the division of Being into whatness and thatness by inquiring into the common element that determines what is divided. What is it that still remains as "–is" if we disregard the what and the that? But if this search for what is most general leads to emptiness, must whatness be grasped as a kind of thatness or, on the contrary, must the latter be grasped as a degeneration of the former? Even if this were successful, the question about the origin of the distinction would still remain. Does it come from Being itself? What "is" Being? How does the coming of the distinction, its origin, result from Being? Or is this distinction merely attributed to Being? If so, by what kind of thinking and by what right? How is Being given to such *at*tribution for such attribution?

If the questions raised are thought through even roughly, the illusion of being a matter of course, in which the distinction of essentia *and* existentia *stands for all metaphysics, disappears.* The distinction is groundless if metaphysics simply tries again and again to define the limits of what is divided, and comes up with numbering the manners of possibility and the kinds of actuality which float away into vagueness, together with the difference in which they are already placed.

However, if it is true that metaphysics accounts for its essence through this difference, obscure in origin, of the what and the that, and grounds its essence thereupon, it can never of itself come to a knowledge of this distinction. It would have to be previously and as such approached by Being which has entered this distinction. But Being refuses this approach, and thus alone makes possible the essential beginning of metaphysics—in the manner of the preparation and development of this distinction. The origin of the distinction of *essentia* and *existentia,* for more so the origin of Being thus divided, remains concealed, expressed in the Greek manner: forgotten.

Oblivion of Being means: the self-concealing of the origin of

Being divided into whatness and thatness in favor of Being which opens out beings as beings and remains unquestioned *as Being.*

The division into whatness and thatness does not just contain a doctrine of metaphysical thinking. It points to an event in the history of Being. This is what must be thought about. It is not sufficient for such recollection to trace the common distinction between *essentia* and *existentia* to its origin in the thinking of the Greeks. And it is not at all sufficient "to explain," that is, to account for the ground in terms of its consequences, the distinction which became decisive in Greek thinking with the help of the subsequent conceptual formulation common to the metaphysics of the schoolmen. It is, of course, easy to establish historically the connection of the distinction between *essentia* and *existentia* with the thinking of Aristotle, who first brought the distinction to a concept, that is, at the same time to its essential ground. This occurred after Plato's thinking had responded to the claim of Being in a way that prepared that distinction by bringing its establishment out into the open.

Essentia answers the question *ti estin:* what is (a being)? *Existentia* says of a being *hoti estin:* that it is. The distinction names a different *estin.* Being *(einai)* announces itself in a difference. How can Being come apart in this distinction? What essence of Being reveals itself in this distinction as in the openness of that essence?

In the beginning of its history, Being opens itself out as emerging *(physis)* and unconcealment *(aletheia).* From there it reaches the formulation of presence and permanence in the sense of enduring *(ousia).* Metaphysics proper begins with this.

What presence appears in presencing? What becomes present shows itself to Aristotle's thinking as that which stands in a permanence having come to a stand, or lies present having been brought to its place. The permanent lying-present which has come forward to unconcealment is in each case this and that, a *tode ti.* Aristotle understands what is permanent and lying present as something somehow at rest. Rest turns out to be a quality of presence. But rest is an eminent way of being moved. Motion completes itself in rest.

What is moved is brought to the stand and position of a presencing (verbal), brought in a bringing-forth. This can occur in the manner of *physis* (allowing something to emerge of itself) or in the manner of *poiesis* (to produce and represent something). The presence of presencing, whether it is something at rest or in motion, receives its essential determination when motion and, with it, rest as fundamental characteristics of Being originating from presencing are understood as one of its modes.

In his "Physics," Aristotle distinguishes being in motion and being at rest as characteristics of presence and interprets these characteristics in terms of the primordially decisive essence of Being, in the sense of emergent presencing in what is unconcealed.

The house standing there *is exposed* in unconcealment in that it is established in its outward appearance and stands in this appearance. Standing, it rests, rests in the "ex" of its exposure. The resting of what is produced is not nothing, but rather gathering. It has gathered into itself all the movements of the production of the house, terminated them in the sense of completed boundary—*peras, telos*—not in the sense of mere cessation. Rest preserves the completion of what is moved. The house there *is* as *ergon*. "Work" means what is completely at rest in the rest of outward appearance—standing, lying in it—what is completely at rest in presencing in unconcealment.

Thought in the Greek manner, the work is not work in the sense of the accomplishment of a strenuous making. It is also not result and effect. It is a work in the sense of that which is placed in the unconcealment of its outward appearance and endures thus standing or lying. To endure means here: to be present at rest as work.

Ergon now characterizes the manner of presencing. Presence, *ousia*, thus means *energeia:* to presence-as-work (presence understood verbally) in the work of work-ness. Workness does not mean actuality as the result of an action, but rather the presencing, standing there in unconcealment, of what is set up. Thus *energeia,* thought in the Greek manner, also has nothing to do with the so-called energy of later times. At best the opposite is true, but only in a very remote sense. Instead of *energeia*, Aristotle also uses the word *entelecheia* which he himself coined. *Telos* is the end in which the movement of producing and setting up gathers itself. This gathering portrays the presencing of what is completed and ended, that is, of what is fulfilled (the work). *Entelecheia* is having-(itself)-in-the-end, the containing of presencing which leaves all production behind and is thus immediate, pure: being in presence. *Energeia, entelecheia on* means the same as *en to eidei einai*. What presences in virtue of "being-in-the-work-as-work" has its present in its outward appearance and through its outward appearance. *Energeia* is the *ousia* (presence) of the *tode ti*, of the this and the that *in each case*.

As this presence, *ousia* is called: *to eschaton*, the presence in which presencing contains its utmost and ultimate. This highest manner of presence also grants the first and nearest presence of everything which in each case lingers as this and as that in unconcealment. If *einai* 9being) has thus determined the highest manner of its presencing as *energeia*, then *ousia* thus determined must also of its own show how it can separate into the differentiation of whatness and thatness, and also must thus separate in consequence of the eminent prevailing of Being as *energeia*.

The distinction of a twofold *ousia* (presence) has become necessary. The beginning of the fifth chapter of Aristotle's treatise on the "categories" expresses this distinction.

Ousia de estin he kuriotata te kai protos kas malista legomene, he mete kath'hypokeimenou tinos legetai mete en hypokeimeno tini estin, hoion ho tis anthropos e ho tis hippos.

"What is present in the sense of predominantly presencing (presence) which is thus predicated firstly and for the most part is that which is predicated neither with respect to something already before us, nor (first) occurs in something already before us, for example, the man there, the horse there."[1]

---

1. Cf. Ross translation: "Substance, in the truest and primary and most definite

What presences in such a way is not a possible predicate, nothing presencing in or with another.

Presence in the eminent and primal sense is the persisting of something which lingers of itself, lies present, the persisting of the individual in each case, the *ousia* of the *kath'hekaston:* The This, The singular.

In terms of presence thus defined, the other presence is distinguished whose presencing is thus characterized: *deuterai de ousiai legontai, en hois eidesin hai protos ousiai legomenai hyparchousin, tauta te kai ta ton eidon touton gene: hoion ho tis anthropos en eidei men hyparchei to anthropo, genos de tou eidous esti to zoon. deuterai oun hautai legontai ousiai, hoion ho te anthropos kai to zoon. (Categ.* V, 2a 11 ff.) "What is present in the second degree, however, are those (notice the plural) in which that which is spoken about as presence in the first degree (as such in each case) already dominates as in the manner of outward appearance. The (named) manners of outward appearance and also the origins of these modes belong here; for example, this man stands there in the outward appearance of a man, but for this outward appearance 'man,' the origin (of his outward appearance) is 'the living being.' Thus what is present in the second degree are these: for example, 'man' (in general) and also 'the living being' (in general.)"[2] Presence in the secondary sense is the showing itself of outward appearance to which all origins also belong, in which what actually persists allows that as which it presences to emerge.

Presence in the primary sense is Being which is expressed in the *hoti estin:* that something is, *existentia.* Presence in the secondary

---

sense of the word, is that which is neither predicable of a subject nor present in a subject; for instance, the individual man or horse."—All footnotes in this book have been supplied by the translator. Appreciation is expressed to Frank Oveis for his assistance in translating Latin passages.

2. Ibid.: "But in a secondary sense those things are called substances within which, as species, the primary substances are included; also those which, as genera, include the species. For instance, the individual man is included in the species 'man', and the genus to which that species belongs is 'animal'; these, therefore—that is to say, the species 'man' and the genus 'animal'—are termed secondary substances."

sense is Being, to which we trace back in the *ti estin:* what something is, *essentia.*

That something is and what something is are revealed as modes of presencing whose fundamental characteristic is *energeia.*

But doesn't a quite different, more far-reaching distinction underlie the difference of *hoti estin* and *ti estin,* namely that of what presences and presencing? In this case, the difference as such first named lies on one side of the distinction of beings and Being. The *hoti estin* and the *ti estin* name manners of presencing to the extent that what is present in them presences in the lasting of each thing or else remains hidden in the mere showing itself of outward appearance. The distinction between what something is and that it is comes from Being (presence) itself. For presencing has within itself the difference of the pure nearness of lasting and of levels of being in the origins of outward appearance. But how does presencing have this *difference within itself?*

As familiarly as the distinction of *essentia* and *existentia* together with the difference of Being and beings offers itself for thinking, the essential origin of these differences is just as obscure, and the structure of their belonging together just as indefinite. Perhaps metaphysical thinking in accordance with its essence can produce no understanding for the enigmatic character of these differences which are a matter of course for it.

Nevertheless, since Aristotle thinks *ousia* (presence) in the primary sense as *energeia* and since this presence means nothing other than what in a changed interpretation is later called *actualitas,* "actuality" and "existence" and "reality," the Aristotelian treatment of the distinction reveals a priority of the later so-called *existentia* over the *essentia.* What Plato thought as the true, and for him sole, beingness *(ousia)* of beings, presence in the manner of *idea (eidos),* now moves to the secondary rank within Being. For Plato, the essence of Being gathers itself in the *koinon* of the *idea,* and thus in the *hen* which, however, is determined as the unifying One by *physis* and *logos,* that is, by the gathering allowing-to-emerge. For Aristotle,

Being consists in the *energeia* of the *tode ti*. In terms of *energeia*, *eidos* can be thought as a manner of presencing. In contrast, the *tode ti*, the actual being, is incomprehensible in its beingness when thought in terms of *idea*. (The *tode ti* is a *me on*—and yet an *on*.)

Still, the historical relationship of Aristotle to Plato is established even today by explanations, variously nuanced, as follows: In contradistinction to Plato, who held that the "Ideas" were "what is truly existent," allowed for individual beings only as seeming beings *(eidolon)*, and demoted them to that which really ought not to be called beings *(me on)*, Aristotle took the free-floating "Ideas" back from their "supraheavenly place" and planted them in actual things. In doing this, Aristotle thought the "Ideas" as "forms" and conceived these "forms" as "energies" and "forces" housed in beings.

This curious explanation, inevitable in the progression of metaphysics, of the relationship between Plato and Aristotle with regard to the thinking of the Being of beings calls forth two questions: How should Aristotle be able at all to bring the Ideas down to actual beings if he has not in advance conceived the individual actual being *as* that which truly presences? But how should he reach the concept of the individual real being's presence, if he doesn't previously think the Being of beings in the sense of the primordially decided essence of Being in terms of presencing in unconcealment? Aristotle does not transplant the Ideas (as if they were things) into individual things. Rather, he thinks for the first time the individual as the actual, and thinks its lasting as the distinctive manner of presencing, of the presencing of *eidos* itself in the most extreme present of the indivisible, that is, no longer derived, appearance *(atomon eidos)*.

The same essence of Being, presencing, which Plato thinks for the *koinon* in the *idea*, is conceived by Aristotle for the *tode ti* as *energeia*. In that Plato can never admit the individual being as what is truly in being, and in that Aristotle, however, conceives the individual together with presencing, Aristotle is more truly Greek in his thinking than Plato, that is, more in keeping with the primordially decided essence of Being. Still, Aristotle was able to think *ousia* as *energeia* only in opposition to *ousia* as *idea,* so that he also keeps *eidos* as subordinate presence in the essential constitution of the presencing of what is present. However, to say that Aristotle is more truly Greek in his thinking than Plato in the way described does not mean that he again comes closer to the primordial thinking of Being. Between *energeia* and the primordial essence of Being *(aletheia–physis)* stands the *idea.*

Both modes of *ousia, idea* and *energeia,* form in the interplay of their distinction the fundamental structure of all metaphysics, of all truth of beings as such. Being announces its essence in these two modes:

Being is presence as the showing itself of outward appearance. Being is the lasting of the actual being in such outward appearance. This double presence in-sists upon presence, and thus becomes present as constancy: enduring, lasting.

The two modes can be thought only by saying each time, from the vantage point of beings relative back to beings, what they are and that they are. Within its history as "metaphysics," Being limits its truth (unconcealing) to what is in being in the sense of *idea* and *energeia. Energeia* takes precedence without, however, ever being able to repress *idea* as a fundamental characteristic of Being.

The pro-gression—to be taken here in its literal meaning—of metaphysics from its beginning, which Plato and Aristotle ground, consists in the fact that these first metaphysical determinations of presence change and also draw the mode of their mutual distinction into this change. Finally, their distinction disappears in a peculiar confounding.

THE CHANGE OF ENERGEIA TO ACTUALITAS

The pro-gression of metaphysics from its essential beginning leaves this beginning behind, and yet takes a fundamental constituent of Platonic-Aristotelian thinking along. This tradition, of which metaphysics itself retains knowledge and later on specifically reports upon in a historical manner, gives rise to the illusion that the transformation which pro-gressed from the essential beginning of metaphysics is the preservation of the genuine fundamental constituents and at the same time its progressive development. This illusion has its real support in the opinion, which has long since become public property, that the fundamental concepts of metaphysics remain everywhere the same.

Idea becomes idea, and this becomes representational thought. *Energeia* becomes *actualitas,* and this becomes actuality. Even though the linguistic formulations of the essential constituents of Being change, the constituents, so it is said, remain the same. If changing fundamental positions of metaphysical thinking develop on this foundation, then their manifoldness only confirms the unchanging unity of the underlying determinations of Being. However, this unchangingness is only an illusion under whose protection metaphysics occurs as history of Being.

In this history, the two differentiated modes of Being, whatness as *idea* and thatness as *energeia,* each assumes a different criterion for the manner in which Being holds itself in the determination of what is in being. When it becomes valid as Being, whatness encourages the predominance of looking at *what* beings are, and thus makes possible a peculiar precedence of beings. Thatness, in which nothing seems to be said about beings themselves (about their "what"), is enough to establish that beings are, whereby the "is" and Being thought in that "is" are simply taken for granted. When it becomes valid as Being, thatness makes it possible that the essence of Being is assumed as self-evident. *Both factors, the precedence of beings and the assumed self-evidence of Being, characterize metaphysics.* Because thatness remains unquestioned everywhere in its *nature,* not, however, with regard to actual beings (whether they are or are not), the unified essence of Being, Being as the unity of whatness and thatness, also determines itself tacitly from what is unquestioned.

Thus the history of Being is primarily revealed in the history of *energeia* which is later called *actualitas* and *existentia,* actuality and existence. But is actuality only the translation for the same essence of *energeia* retained in its sameness? And does *existentia* preserve that fundamental characteristic of Being which in general received its form in *ousia* (presence)? *Ex-sistere speculo* means for Cicero to step out of the cave. One might suspect here a deeper relation of *existentia* as stepping out and forward to coming forward to presence and unconcealment. Then the Latin word *existentia* would preserve an essential Greek content. That is not the case. Similarly, *actualitas* no longer preserves the essence of *energeia.* The literal translation is misleading. In truth it brings precisely another transposition or misplacement to the word of Being. This transposition of another type of humanity to the whole of beings occurs by virtue of the closure of Being. The character of that-*being* and of the "that" has changed.

In the beginning of metaphysics, beings as *ergon* are what presence in their being produced. Now *ergon* becomes the *opus* of the *operari,* the *factum* of the *facere,* the *actus* of the *agere.* The *ergon* is no longer what is freed in the openness of presencing, but rather what is effected in working, what is accomplished in action. The essence of the "work" is no longer "workness" in the sense of distinctive presencing in the open, but rather the "reality" of a real thing which rules in working and is fitted into the procedure of working. Having progressed from the beginning essence of *energeia,* Being has become *actualitas.*

Thus in the horizon of historical description, a transition from the Greek to the Roman conceptual language has come about. But in order to realize sufficiently even merely historically the scope of this transition, the Roman character must be understood in the full wealth of its historical developments, so that it includes the politically imperial element of Rome, the Christian element of the Roman church, and the Romantic element as well. With a peculiar fusion of imperial and papal elements, the Romantic becomes the origin of that fundamental structure of the modernly experienced

reality called *cultura* ("culture"), and for various reasons was unknown to the Greeks and the Romans, and to the German medieval
period as well.

When counted in epochs, the determination of Being as *actualitas* thus extends throughout the whole of Western history from
the Romans up until the most recent of modern times. Because the
essential determination of Being as *actualitas* underlies all history in
advance, that is, at the same time the structure of relationships of
a certain type of humanity to beings as a whole, all Western history
since is in a manifold sense Roman, and never Greek. Every subsequent reawakening of Greek antiquity is a Roman renovation of
that Greece already reinterpreted in a Roman way. The Germanic
character of the medieval period, too, is Roman in its metaphysical
essence, because it is Christian. Ever since the transformation of
energeia to *actualitas* (reality), the real is truly what is in being and
thus decisive for everything possible and necessary.

But Being as *actualitas* is in itself historical, in that it accomplishes the truth of its essence and in that it thus makes possible the
fundamental positions of metaphysics. The distinction at the beginning maintains itself in Being throughout: *Actualitas* is differentiated as *existentia* from *potentia (possibilitas)* as *essentia*. *Actualitas*
preserves nothing of the essence of *energeia* over and above the
indefinite relation to the work. And yet the essence of Being at its
beginning still prevails in *actualitas*, too, since whatness is determined as *idea*. The fundamental characteristic of *idea* (cf. "Plato's
Doctrine of Truth," 1942) is the *agathon*. Outward appearance
showing itself makes beings capable of becoming present as this and
that. *Idea* as whatness has the character of *aitia*, cause. Origination
from its whatness dominates in every coming-to-be of beings. Whatness is the matter of every thing, that is, its cause. Accordingly,
Being is in itself causal.

As a consequence of the Platonic determination of Being as
idea, that is, as *agathon*, the decisive role of *aitia* unfolds in the
essence of Being. Here the character of being-responsible-for as

making possible does not necessarily and exclusively have the character of effective working. Still, the precedence of *aitia* gets so firmly fixed in the beginning of metaphysics that it takes over the place of the premetaphysical determination of Being as *arche;* more exactly: it brings about the transformation of the character of *arche* to that of *aition.* Soon the equation of *arche* and *aitia,* in part already with Aristotle, becomes a matter of course. Being shows the essential characteristic of the making possible of presence, that is, of effecting constancy or permanence. Thus, in spite of the gap between *energeia* and *actualitas,* the transformation to Being as *esse actu* is prepared from the metaphysical essence of Being at its beginning, too.

When Being has changed to *actualitas* (reality), beings are what is real. They are determined by working, in the sense of causal making. The reality of human action and divine creation can be explained in terms of this. Being which has changed to *actualitas* gives to beings as a whole that fundamental characteristic which the representational thinking of the biblical-Christian faith in creation can take over in order to secure metaphysical justification for itself. Conversely, through the dominance of the Christian-ecclesiastical interpretation of beings, the fundamental position of Being as reality attains an assumed self-evidence which has remained decisive ever since for all subsequent understanding of the beingness of beings, even apart from the attitude of strict faith and its scholarly interpretation of beings as a whole. The predominance of the determination of Being as reality, now immediately comprehensible to everyone, gets firmly fixed so that soon, conversely, *energeia* is understood in terms of *actualitas,* and the primordial Greek essential character of Being is once and for all misunderstood and made inaccessible by the Roman interpretation of Being. The tradition of the truth about beings which goes under the title of "metaphysics" develops into a pile of distortions, no longer recognizing itself, covering up the primordial essence of Being. Herein lies the reason for the necessity of the "destruction" of this distortion, when a thinking of the truth of being has become necessary (cf. *Being and Time*). But this destruction, like "phenomenology" and all her-meneutical-transcendental questions, has not yet been thought in terms of the history of Being.

Real beings are what truly is, because actuality constitutes the true essence of thatness; for actuality thought as *energeia* is the fulfilled presence of the actual being. But the more the presencing being endures in a lasting manner, the more actual it remains.

Esse, in contradistinction to *essentia,* is *esse actu. Actualitas,* however, is *causalitas.* The causal character of Being as reality shows itself in all purity in that being which fulfills the essence of Being in the highest sense, since it is that being which can never not be. Thought "theologically," this being is called "God." It doesn't know the state of possibility because in that state it would not yet be something. In every not-yet there lies a lack of Being, in that Being is distinguished by permanence. The highest being is pure actuality always fulfilled, *actus purus.* Effecting is here the persisting presencing of itself of what persists for itself. This being *(ens)* is not only what it is *(sua essentia),* but in what it is, it is always also the persistence of what it is *(est suum esse non participans alio).* For this reason, metaphysically thought, God is called the *summum ens.* The apex of his Being, however, consists in his being the *summum bonum.* For the *bonum* is *causa,* and as *finis* the *causa causarum.* Thus, precisely with respect to *causalitas* (that is, *actualitas*) the *bonum* is what gives persistence to everything that persists and is thus *prius quam ens; causalitas causae finalis est prima.*

There is not a moral characterization or even an idea of "value" contained in the statement *"Deus est summum bonum."* The name *summum bonum* is rather the purest expression for the causality which is appropriate to the purely real, in accordance with its effectuating the persistence of everything that can persist (cf. Thomas Aquinas, *Summa theol.* I, qu. 1–23). Ontologically understood, the *bonum* thought with regard to the *summum ens* is the echo of the Platonic *agathon,* that is, what absolutely makes capable, namely for beings as such—what makes possible: the condition of possibility (cf. "Plato's Doctrine of Truth").

But also in the *actualitas,* which is determined in every respect by *causalitas,* the essence of beingness at the beginning maintains itself in a changed form: presence. The *summum ens* is distinctively characterized by *omnipraesentia.* However, "ubiquity," (to be present everywhere) is also determined "causally." *Deus est ubique per essentiam* inquantum *adest omnibus* ut causa essendi (qu. 8a, 3).

The interpretation of *existentia* can also be explained by the causal character of reality. This is the name for the other concept which is mostly equated in meaning with *actualitas* (reality), and is even used far more often in the conceptual language of metaphysics, above all in the distinction of *essentia* and *existentia* ("essence" and "existence"). The origin of the word *existentia* is traced back to two passages in Aristotle's *Metaphysics* which both treat almost identically the *on hos alethes,* the Being of beings in the sense of "unconcealed" (*Met.* E 4, 1027b 17 and *Met.* K 8, 1065a 21ff.). Here Aristotle speaks about a *exo ousa tis physis tou ontos* and about the *exo on kai choriston.* The *exo,* outside, means the Outside *tes dianoias,* that is, human reason which permeates beings in discussion, and in doing so establishes what it has talked about. What is established in this way consists and presences only for such discussion and in the neighborhood of its activity. What is outside *(exo)* consists and stands as something persisting in itself in its own place *(choriston).* What thus "stands outside," *ex-sistens,* the ex-isting, is nothing other than what presences of itself in its being produced, the *on energeia.*

At this point, a derivation of the Latin word *ex-sistentia* from an Aristotelian explanation of beings is called for. More important for insight into the history of Being is the fact that the characterization of what presences of itself *(ousia)* is already based upon a changed essence of truth. The "true" is still called *alethes,* the unconcealed; but what is true, namely the proposition, is true not because it itself as revealing is something "unconcealed," but rather because it establishes and thinks what is unconcealed by the adequation of reason. The determination of Being in the sense of *ex-sistentia* as

Aristotle thought it originates in that change of the essence of truth from the unconcealment of beings to the correctness of the reasoned proposition. This change already begins with Plato and underlies the beginning of metaphysics. Although this origin, which is likewise already metaphysical, echoes indefinitely enough in the concept *ex-sistentia*, too, *ex-sistentia* receives its decisive meaning from *actualitas*, that is, with regard to *causalitas*.

In his *Disputationes metaphysicae* (XXXI, sect. IV n. 6), whose influence continuing into the beginning of modern metaphysics has meanwhile become more evident, Suarez says this about *ex-sistentia*: *nam esse existentiae nihil aliud est quam illud esse, quo formaliter, et immediate entitas aliqua constituitur extra causas suas, et desinit esse nihil, ac incipit esse aliquid: sed huiusmodi est hoc esse quo formaliter et immediate constituitur res in actualitate essentiae: ergo est verum esse existentiae.* [3]

Existence is that Being through which a being is truly and immediately established outside of the causes with the result that nonbeing ceases, and an actual being begins to be. *Ex-sistentia* is related in each case to one being in accordance with the underlying distinction in Being. What a being is in each case is established by existence in the sphere outside of causality. This means: Whatness undergoes a causal realization in such a way that what is thus produced is released as a product from causality, and established on its own basis as something real. The "extra" is no longer related like the Aristotelian *exo* to the *dianoia*, to human reason, but rather to a transpiring causality. *Ex-sistentia* is *actualitas* in the sense of the *res extra causes et nihilum sistentia*, a production which transposes something into the realm outside of causality and actuality, the realm of being produced, and thus overcomes nothingness (that is, the lack of real beings).

But if *ex-sistentia* is placed in the realm outside of causality, how

---

3. "For the being of existence is nothing but that being by which some entity is formally and immediately established outside of its causes, and ceases to be nothing, and begins to be something: And indeed of such a kind is this being by which a thing is formally and immediately established in the actuality of essence: Therefore it is the true being of existence."

can *actualitas* still determine the essence of existence? Is not existence the taking leave of causality? On the contrary. In that existence exposes from the area of causality to the openness of working, which is now a real being based upon itself and thus an effective being, existence is precisely dependent upon causality. Placing and establishing, the making-stand of *ex-sistentia*, is what it is *out of* causality, but only out of *it*. The *ex-sistentia* is the *actus, quo res sistitur, ponitur extra statum possibilitatis*. It alone can and should *ex-pose* from the cause the thing as caused, that is, produced.

The usual name for thatness, existence, testifies to the precedence of Being as *actualitas* in this interpretation. The dominance of its essence as *reality* determines the progression of the history of Being, throughout which the essential determination once begun is carried out to its prefigured completion. The real is the existing. The existing includes everything which through some manner of causality *constituitur extra causas*. But because the whole of beings is the effected and effecting product of a first producer, an appropriate structure enters the whole of beings which determines itself as the co-responding of the actual produced being to the producer as the highest being. The reality of the grain of sand, of plants, animals, men, numbers, co-responds to the making of the first maker. It is at the same time like and unlike his reality. The thing which can be experienced and grasped with the senses is existent, but so is the object of mathematics which is nonsensuous and calculable. "M exists" means: this quantity can be unequivocally constructed from an established point of departure of calculation with established methods of calculation. What is thus constructed is thus proven as something effective within a context of calculative proof. "M" is something with which one can calculate, and under certain conditions must calculate. Mathematical construction is a kind of constitution of the *constituere extra causas*, of causal effecting.

Being is given in the essence of reality, and reality determines the existence of what exists. Being presences as effecting in the unified-manifold sense according to which what effects, but also what is effected and also what is the effected-effecting and the effective being, is what-is. The being thus determined in a manifold way in virtue of effecting is *real*.

It can only be recollected that Being has been given to the essence of reality. Recollection points back to the previous essence of Being in the sense of worklike and visible presencing. The progression out of this essence allows the *agathon* and the *aition* to become determining.

The essential origin of Being as making possible and as causing rules throughout the future history of Being. Making possible, causing, accounting for are determined in advance as gathering in virtue of the One as what is uniquely unifying. This unifying is neither an intertwining nor an assembling. The *hen* in which the essence of Being rests has the character of concealing-unconcealing, of the gathering to be thought. The unity of the One is shown throughout the history of Being in various forms whose differences stem from the change of essence of *aletheia*, of concealing-unconcealing.

If as a consequence of this event beings have meanwhile long since and generally been experienced and have been the subject of opinion, this opining can still never encroach upon the strange uniqueness of even this essence of Being. The opining about Being as reality does veil the event of this essential origin. But opining can never harm the decisiveness in virtue of which this essence of Being brings the progression of its history to its utmost completion.

The transformation of truth to certainty

The hidden history of Being as reality also first makes possible Western man's various *fundamental positions* within beings. These fundamental positions ground in each case the truth about Being on the basis of what is real and establish and make this truth certain for what is real. Even though the essence of Being as reality fixates as ultimate an irrevocable change in the face of worklike presence *(energeia)*, still the question of how effecting and reality are determined remains open within the essential realm thus decided. In accordance with the precedence of beings which starts with the beginning of metaphysics, Being, meanwhile represented as the general determination *(koinon, katholou, genus, commune)* of beings, takes its essential shape in virtue of an authoritative being.

What real being the authoritative effecting effects as the determination of reality's essence cannot be calculated and can only be seemingly established historically. Since the creator god as first cause is what primarily effects, and since his effects, however, are the world, and within the world the true effector is man; the triad: God, world (nature), man circumscribes the realm of possibilities according to which one of these realms of what is real takes over the structuring of reality's essence. Assuming, however, that the determination of reality in accordance with what is authoritatively real also does not primordially come from beings, but rather stems from Being itself; then the development of reality's essence within a metaphysics must also point to this origin. An indication of this becomes apparent in the fact that the actual essence of truth, in whose light a period of mankind experiences beings, participates in the history of Being. The manner of this participation remains, of course, profoundly veiled.

Truth, meanwhile in metaphysics changed to the distinctive trait of the intellect *(humanus, divinus)*, comes to its ultimate essence which is called *certainty*. The name expresses the fact that truth concerns consciousness as a knowledge, a representation which is grounded in consciousness in such a way that only that knowledge is valid as knowledge which at the same time knows itself and what it knows as such, and is certain of itself in this knowledge. Certainty here is not to be taken only as an addition to knowledge in the sense that it accomplishes the appropriation and the possession of knowledge. Rather, certainty is the authoritative mode of knowledge, that is, "truth," as the consciousness, conscious of itself, of what is known. The mere having of something in consciousness is, in contrast, either no longer knowledge or not yet knowledge.

That truth becomes certainty in essence is an event whose beginning is inaccessible to all metaphysics. On the other hand, in connection with this essential change of truth, a peculiar preeminence of humanity within what is real soon becomes evident, and at the same time, however, also a corresponding role of what is unconditionally real, thought in a theological manner. As knowing beings, both realities, God and man, are metaphysically the bearers of truth and thus constitute the reality of knowledge and certainty.

However, it lies in the essence of certainty to be certain of itself in each case, that is, to claim for itself the final assurance of itself. Certainty thus first and alone determines the reality of what is real, which at first appears to be only its actual support. By thus exhibiting its support in terms of the essential claim to the self-accomplishment of its self-assuring, it kindles the battle between the possible supports of its essence. Before all, the creator god, and with him the institution of the offering and management of his gifts of grace (the church), is in sole possession of the sole and eternal truth. As *actus purus,* God is pure actuality and thus the causality of everything real, that is, the source and the place of salvation which as blessedness guarantees eternal permanence. By himself, man can never become, and be, absolutely certain of this salvation. On the other hand, through faith and similarly through lack of faith, man is essentially established in the attainment of salvation's certainty, or forced to the renunciation of this salvation and its certainty. Thus a necessity rules, hidden in its origin, that man make sure of his salvation in some fashion in the Christian or in another sense (salvation: *soteria:* redemption: release).

The origin, belonging to the history of Being, of the dominance of truth as certainty is concealed in the *release* of its essence from the primal truth of Being. Assurance of himself and of his effectiveness determines the reality of man. The possibility is contained here of man's determining the essence of certainty by himself in accordance with the essence of certainty in general (self-assurance), and thus of bringing humanity to dominance within what is real. Man builds upon and builds up of himself what is real as what has an effect upon him and as what he effects. What is real becomes what can be effected within that human activity which, knowingly basing itself upon itself, cultivates everything and takes care of it.

Thus "culture" begins historically as the structure of humanity which is certain of itself and intent upon the assurance of itself (cf. Descartes, *Discours de la méthode*). Culture as such is elevated to the "goal," or, what is essentially the same, it can be set up as the means and value of humanity's dominance over the earth. The Christian church attains a position of protective defense. The decisive action of this defense consists in taking over the stance of this new adversary, who at first still moves and establishes himself within the Christian world. The Christian church becomes Christianity of culture. Conversely, however, culture, that is, the self-certainty of humanity which has become assured of its effectiveness, strives to fit Christianity into its world and to incorporate the truth of Christianity into the certainty of humanity certain of itself and of its possibilities for knowledge.

In that truth becomes the certainty of knowledge of humanity making sure of itself, that history begins which is called the *modern period* in the historical calculation of epochs. The name says more than it means. It says something essential about this age. In that the truth in which its humanity stands demands the development of the assurance of absolute dominance, this essence of truth delivers man and his effecting over to the inevitable and never ceasing worry of increasing the possibilities of safety and making sure of them again in the face of newly enkindled dangers. Man and his effecting advance in the continually new elements of his successes and discoveries, in the continually newest elements of his attainments and conquests, in the continually unheard of elements of his experiences.

This attainment of safety and this arrangement of what is real in safety is able to dominate the historical movement of modern humanity only because the relation of man to everything real changes in the premonitory beginning of this history, in that the truth of beings has become certainty, and certainty since then is developing its own essential fullness as the authoritative essence of truth. But this change of the essence of truth from the correctness of the thinking proposition to the certainty of representational thinking, too, is determined as reality by the *essence of Being.* Thus the change of essence of truth gives an indication for the way in which Being itself begins to complete its essence as reality.

What is truly real *(actus purus)* is God. Reality *(actualitas)* is the effecting causality which of itself brings about the stabilizing of independent constancy. Causality, however, is not exhausted in the effectuation of the constancy on earth of all that is not divine, that is, created. The highest causality is the *actus purus* as *summum bonum,* which as the final goal *(finis)* predestining everything and thus elevating everything to its true constancy anchors all reality of what is real in the first cause. For this reason, that real being which is man, created in the image of God, must above all bring about his reality by holding fast to the highest good, that is, by faith *(fides, qua creditur).* Through faith, man is certain of the reality of the highest real being, and thus at the same time also of his own real continuance in eternal bliss. The causality of the highest real being allots to man thus created a definite kind of reality whose fundamental characteristic is faith.

In faith rules certainty, that kind of certainty which is safe even in the uncertainty of itself, that is, of what it believes in. What is believed in is that real being whose reality as *actus purus* binds and directs all human activity in its plans and ideas. Man can stand in such a commitment only if he of himself and as himself bows down toward something committing him, frees himself for what he believes in such bowing down, and is free in such a way. Man's freedom ruling in faith and its certainty *(propensio in bonum* cf. Descartes, *Meditationes de prima philosophia* IV, "De vero et falso")* develops as the essential structure of created man only when all human behavior, in its own way, bears within itself that fundamental character in relation to everything real, in its own way, which as certainty presents and assures what is real to effecting man in each case.

Man, however, does not just relate through *faith* to God and to the world created by God. Man also relates to what is real through the *lumen naturale.* In the natural light of reason, a certainty native to him must become authoritative if certainty decides about the adequate relation to what is real. All natural human behavior and action must necessarily be completely based upon a certainty which man has brought about for himself if the supranatural is grounded in natural behavior in some way in accordance with the principle: *gratia supponit naturam.* The essence of truth of man's natural behavior must be certainty.

This demand for the self-protection of his natural constancy accomplished by man himself does not come from a revolt against the doctrine of faith. On the contrary, it is the necessary consequence of the fact that the highest truth has the character of the certainty of salvation. The essential transformation of truth to the certainty of representational thinking is determined by the essence of Being as *actus purus.* For this reason, the world of Christian faith remains authoritative throughout manifold transformations for the organization and cultivation of what is real (for culture) in the history of the modern period, but it is also authoritative for the interpretation of what is real in terms of its reality (for modern metaphysics). Modern culture is Christian even when it loses its faith. On the other hand, Christianity tries in all ways to remain capable of being cultural and to be a Christianity of culture, most of all where the Christianity of faith is furthest removed from original Christianity.

If the natural ideas, brought about by man himself, about what is real are thus supported and guided by truth as certainty, every real being placed in a truth, every true being *(ens verum)* must be an *ens certum: "ac proinde jam videor pro regula generali posse statuere, illud omne esse verum, quod valde clare et distincte percipio.*" (Descartes, *Meditatio* III.)[4]

Something true is that which man of himself clearly and distinctly brings before himself and confronts as what is thus brought before him (re-presented) in order to guarantee what is represented in such a confrontation. The assurance of such representation is certainty. What is true in the sense of being certain is what is real. The essence of the reality of what is real lies in the constancy and continuity of what is represented in the certain representation. This constancy excludes the inconstancy of the wavering common to all representational thinking as long as it doubts. Representational thinking which is free of doubt is clear and distinct thinking. What is thus represented has also already presented what is constant, that is, what is real, to representational thinking.

Reality is representation in the sense of the constancy of the continuous which is set up *by* certain representational thinking and *for* it.

It is true that in the beginning of the essential transformation of reality whose history fulfills modern metaphysics as history of Being, this essence is not yet expressed as such. On the contrary. It almost seems as if in the beginning of modern metaphysics the traditional essence of reality, *actualitas,* is maintained just as it is, and only the manner of *comprehension* of what is real, knowledge, is subjected to a special inquiry ("theory"). The essence of Being in the beginning of modern metaphysics is actually ambiguous in that a manifold of essential possibilities of the essential completion of reality appears which later coalesces, developed from original unity. The ambiguity of the essence of reality in the beginning of modern metaphysics is the sign of a genuine transition. In contrast, the supposed singleness of meaning which is presumably expressed in the *cogito ergo sum* is an illusion.

4. "And accordingly it seems to me that already I can establish as a general rule that all things which I perceive very clearly and very distinctly are true."

Certainty as the essence of truth claims of itself to have a manner, thoroughly adequate for itself, of knowability and of what can be added and built up as truly real through certainty in knowledge, and thus assured in constancy. Certainty is the assurance of everything represented which grounds itself in its own essence and is entrusted to that essence alone. For this reason, certainty requires an underlying support sufficient for *it* which expressly lies continually present for representing as the ground for all representational construction and bringing about of what is real.

If the essence of truth, having become certainty, brings about its adequate relation to what is real through and for man who is placed in the essence of truth by requiring him to construct what is knowable as that which can be produced with certainty; and if the certainty for this construction requires that basis in which certainty's own essence is incorporated as the foundation, then something real must be secured in advance for all representational thinking whose reality, that is, persistence, is removed from every threat to representational thinking in the sense of dubitability. The demand for certainty goes after a *fundamentum absolutum et inconcussum*, a basis which no longer depends upon a relation to something else, but rather is absolved from the very beginning from this relation, and rests within itself.

Which real being is appropriate to be such a basis, in such a way that it can at the same time change to suit the essence of reality (the constancy for all representational thinking) prepared by certainty?

The Transformation of Hypokeimenon to Subiectum

Up to and still during the beginning of the modern period, what is real is the *ens actu*, what effects and is effected in its relative constancy. In contrast, in the beginning of metaphysics, Being presences not as *actualitas* (actuality), but as workness *(energeia)* for which the lasting of the actual suffices. The actual lies present of itself, it is the true *hypokeimenon*. Aristotle calls everything which has come to be along with what is already present the *symbebekota*. In this name, the character of presencing and thus the Greek essence of Being *(ousia)* can still be heard. However, because the *symbebekota* only presence *along with*, only come as an addition to what endures of itself, and only have stability along with it, they are in a certain way a *me on*, something present which does not attain the pure manner of lasting of the actual, the *hypokeimenon*.

In accordance with the change of *energeia* to *actualitas*, the change of *hypokeimenon* to *subiectum* obscures the essence of Being thought in the Greek manner, in spite of the correct translation. The *subiectum* is what is placed and thrown under in the *actus* and can then be joined by other things. In this joining, in the *accidens*, presencing-along-with in presence, that is, a manner of presencing, can no longer be heard. What underlies and has been placed under *(subiectum)* takes over the role of the ground upon which other things are placed so that what has been placed under can also be conceived as what stands under, and thus is constant *before* everything. *Subiectum* and *substans* mean the same thing: what is truly constant and real, what suffices for reality and constancy and is therefore called *substantia*. Soon the essence of *hypokeimenon* determined at the beginning, of what lies present of itself, is interpreted from the perspective of *substantia*. *Ousia*, presence, is thought as *substantia*. The concept of substance is un-Greek, but it dominates together with *actualitas* the essential character of Being in the metaphysics to follow.

However, just as the Aristotelian characterization of *"existens"* is determined as *exo tes dianoias on* through the change of truth from *aletheia* to *homoiosis* and through the concomitant transposition of truth to the proposition *(logos)*, the same essential change of truth and the predominance originating from it of the *kataphasis (logos)* takes over the preparation of a far-reaching ambiguity and reinterpretation of the *hypokeimenon*. Since it is what of itself lies present, what truly is becomes *kath'hou legetai ti*, that of which something shown and stated *(legomenon)* is *predicated* and *attributed* as what is underlying. The *hypokeimenon* is now in turn the *legomenon (logos) kath'hauto*, that which is addressed directly and only as itself, thus becoming accessible as a being. The *logos*, the proposition, now characterizes what underlies as such and signifies what presences of itself, and thus remains the substratum of all predication and negation. Ever since, all essential determinations of beings as such, that is, characterizations of what-is, remain within the confines of the *kataphasis*, that is, of the *kategoria*. They are categories. Because *logos* shapes the essence of what underlies, it becomes the determination of that which *arche* and *aitia* are, of what is later called the underlying ground and cause.

The *"subiectum"* subsequently becomes the name which names the subject in the subject-object relationship, and also the subject in the subject-predicate relationship.

The change of metaphysics at its beginning releases *energeia* into *actualitas, ousia* into the *substantia, aletheia* into the *adaequatio*. Similarly, *logos*, and with it *hypokeimenon*, comes into the sphere of meaning of the translation *ratio (rheo, rhesis* = speech, *ratio; reor* = to predicate, to opine, to justify). *Ratio* is accordingly the other name for *subiectum*, for what underlies. Thus a characterization for human (predicating) behavior comes to play the role of the concept for that which constitutes a being in its true Being, in that as what lasts it is constant in itself, and thus is what stands under all beings, however they may be, the *substantia*. The ground, understood as the essence of the beingness of beings, receives the not-at-all obvious name of *ratio* in subsequent metaphysics.

Everything that endures of itself and thus lies present is *hypokeimenon. Subiectum* is a star and a plant, an animal, a human being and a god. When a *fundamentum absolutum et inconcussum* is required in the beginning of modern metaphysics which as a true being suffices for the essence of truth in the sense of *certitudo cognitionis humanae,* a *subiectum* is being asked for which already lies present in all representing and for all representing, and is what is constant and standing in the sphere of indubitable representational thinking.

Representational thinking *(percipere, co-agitare, cogitare, repraesentare in uno)* is a fundamental characteristic of all human behavior, even of nonepistemological behavior. From this perspective, all behavioral actions are *cogitationes.* However, what constantly already lies present for representational thinking during representation which presents something to itself is the representer itself *(ego cogitans),* before which everything represented is brought, to which and *back* to which *(re-praesentare)* it becomes present. As long as representing continues, the representing *ego cogito* is also expressly what already lies present in representing and for it. Thus the distinctive character of continually already lying present, of the *subiectum,* belongs to the *ego cogito cogitatum* in the sphere of the essential structure of representational thinking *(perceptio).* This constancy is the permanence of that which can never be doubted in any representing, even if this representing is itself a kind of doubting.

The *ego,* the *res cogitans,* is the distinctive *subiectum* whose *esse,* that is, presencing, suffices for the essence of truth in the sense of certainty. This *esse* circumscribes a new essence of the *existentia* which Descartes defines as a *veritas aeterna* (axiom) in section 49 of his *Principia philosophiae* as follows: *is qui cogitat, non potest non existere, dum cogitat.* "Whoever behaves toward something while representing cannot not continually effect while representing.[5]

Reality is characterized as constancy by permanence (the persistence of representational thinking). But at the same time it makes the representing being into an *ens actu.* The effecting of the new essence of reality of this distinctive real being has the fundamental characteristic of representational thinking. Accordingly, the reality of what is represented and added in all representing is characterized by *being represented.*

Thus begins the development of a characteristic of the essence of reality which is later on first conceived by Kant in all clarity as the objectivity of the object. Representational thinking brings about

5. "He who thinks must exist while he thinks."

the presentation of the opposition of the object. As long as we think metaphysically and not, in a manner inappropriate to Being, psychologically, reality as being represented never signifies that what is real is a mental-spiritual product and effect of representational activity, and thus something which only exists as a mental structure. On the contrary, as soon as the fundamental characteristic of representing and being represented comes to power in the essence of reality, the constancy and persistence of what is real is narrowed down to the sphere of presencing in the presence of the *re-praesentatio*. The character of presence prevailing in the metaphysical essence of Being which was not fully obliterated, only changed, even in the transformation of *energeia* to *actualitas* (cf. the *omnipraesentia* of the *actus purus*), now appears as presence within representational thinking *(repraesentatio)*.

Descartes' *Meditations*, which treat the distinction of the *subiectum* man as the *res cogitans*, think Being as the *esse* of the *ens verum qua certum*. The newly thought essence of the reality of what is real is not yet called by a name of its own. This by no means signifies that the *Meditations* turn away from the *Being* of beings to the *knowledge* of beings. For the *Meditations* are characterized as *Meditationes de prima philosophia*, thus as meditations which keep within the sphere of the question about the *ens qua ens*. These *Meditations* are a beginning, indeed a decisive beginning, of the true start of the metaphysics upon which the modern period rests.

But how little the whole conversion to the metaphysics of the modern period is already accomplished here can be seen from the fact that the *res cogitans*, as *fundamentum absolutum et inconcussum* the eminent *subiectum*, is at the same time a *substantia finita*, that is, *creata*, in the sense of traditional metaphysics. The reality of the *substantia finita* is determined by the causality of the *causa prima*. The distinction of the *mens humana* among other *subiecta* is expressed by the fact that it *notior est quam corpus*. This precedence in being known is not a matter of easier comprehensibility, but rather signifies the truer presence of the *res cogitans* in the sphere of human representing as a presenting *to oneself*. Human representing itself and the representing human being are here more constant, more real, and more in being than all other beings when thought from the new essence of reality. In accordance with this distinction of its lying present as *subiectum*, the *mens humana* thus claims in the future the name "subject" exclusively for itself, so that *subiectum* and *ego*, subjectivity and I-ness become equivalent. The "subject" as the name for that about which something is predicated loses its metaphysical dignity in appearance only. This dignity appears in Leibniz and is developed fully in Hegel's *Science of Logic.*

At first, however, all nonhuman beings still remain ambiguous with respect to the essence of their reality. They can be determined by being represented and by objectivity for the representing *subiectum*, but also by the *actualitas* of the *ens creatum* and its substantiality. On the other hand, the sole supremacy of Being as *actualitas* in the sense of the *actus purus* is broken down. Within its metaphysical truth as the beingness of beings, the history of Being begins to bring the various possibilities of its essence to unity, and thus the fulfillment of its essence to completion. It is evident in the earliest beginning of this history that it claims the essence of man with a peculiar decisiveness.

The full beginning of the history of Being in the form of modern metaphysics occurs where the essential completion of Being determined as reality is not yet accomplished as such, but where the possibility of the decisiveness of this completion is totally prepared for, and the ground of the history of completion thus laid. To take upon himself this preparation of the completion of modern metaphysics, and thus everywhere to rule this history of completion, is the determination of the history of Being of that thinking accomplished by Leibniz.

Since the beginning tradition of metaphysics following Aristotle, every true being is a *hypokeimenon*. This *hypokeimenon* is determined afterwards as *subiectum*. Descartes' thinking distinguishes the *subiectum* which man is to the effect that the *actualitas* of this *subiectum* has its essence in the *actus* of *cogitare (percipere).*

But what if the *actualitas* should contain this basic trait of the *percipere* in general? How could it happen that this essential characteristic of the *actualitas* remained concealed? The prevailing essence of truth in each case decides about the manner and the scope of revealedness of the essence of Being. When truth has become certainty, then everything which is truly real must present itself as real to the real being that it is. All effecting is now revealed as a self-effecting in effecting. The essence of this effecting is not fulfilled in the mere effecting of something. All effecting is rather in itself, and not just incidentally, a self-effecting. In effecting lies the essential characteristic which is perhaps most readily named by the expression "coming toward itself," because this expression doesn't anticipate. Effecting is in itself related to itself, and it is only in this relation that it determines its effecting. However, that in relation to which the "coming toward itself" presences does not need to be an I or a self. The "coming toward itself" can be conceived as turning-back *(reflexio)* with regard to the progression of effecting to what is effected. Nevertheless, the question must remain open to where this turning brings back, and what it really represents. Every effecting is an effectuation which brings itself about. By bringing something before itself each time, it accomplishes a presentation and thus represents what is effected in a certain way. Effecting is in itself a representing *(percipere)*. To think the essence of reality more appropriately, more in its own being, now means in the realm of the essence of truth as certainty: to think the essence of the *perceptio* (representation) with regard to the question of how the essence of effecting and reality develops itself more fully from that essence.

Leibniz: the Belonging-together of Reality and Representation

In what way representation, thought sufficiently in an original and complete way, constitutes the fundamental characteristic of the reality of what is real, and thus in what way every being is only truly in being as a representing being, can be seen in the fact that the beingness of beings (the substantiality of substance) and representation are the same, thought from a fundamental determination of beings. This fundamental determination of beings as such is *unity*. Here the ambiguity returns, which runs through all metaphysics, according to which "unity" means the actual "one" determined by unity, but also this determining unity itself. Similarly, *ousia* means a beingness (a being), and Being as the essence of beings.

When Leibniz thinks the "monad," he thinks unity as the essential constitution of "unities." The essential fullness which gives the equivocal title "unity" its precision stems, however, from the belonging together of reality and representational thinking. In a letter of April 30, 1687, to Arnauld (Gerhardt, ed., *Die philosophischen Schriften von G. W. Leibniz*, II, 97), Leibniz says: *"Pour trancher court, je tiens pour un axiome cette proposition identique qui n'est diversifiée que par l'accent, savoir que ce qui n'est pas véritablement un être, n'est pas non plus véritablement un* être."[6] Un *être*, what presences from the actual unifying one; *un* être, a presencing (presence) which as such contains unity. In the letter of June 20, 1703, to de Volder (Gerh. II, 251), we find the sentence: *"Quodsi nullum* vere unum *adest, omnis* vera res *erit sublata.*"[7] What truly unifies produces the presence of every thing.

Unity constitutes the beingness of beings. But this applies only to *true* unity. It consists in an original, that is, simple, unification resting within itself. This unification gathers and enfolds in such a way that what is enfolded is represented and presented to what unifies, and thus at the same time unfolded. *Unity in the sense of this simple enfolding and unfolding unification now has the character of representation.* All representation presents a manifold to the self-con-

6. "In short, I consider as an axiom this identical proposition, which receives two meanings only through a change in accent; namely, that what is not truly *a* being is not truly a *being*."
7. "But if there were no *true one*, then every *true being* would be eliminated."

tained unifying being, and constitutes the state of the one (that is, of the real being). The manifold thus presented is limited in each case in that, granting God as the infinite being, the whole of beings can never be presented in a created being. Every state of the monad produced by representation is thus in itself *in transition* to the next state, and thus essentially transitional. Accordingly, section 14 of the *Monadology* reads (Gerh. VI, 608 ff.): *"L'état passager qui enveloppe et représente une multitude dans l'unité ou dans la substance simple n'est autre chose que ce qu'on appelle la* Perception, *qu'on doit bien distinguer de l'apperception ou de la conscience . . ."*[8] The essence of representation is determined here not psychologically, *but solely with regard to the essence of the beingness of beings,* as their fundamental trait.

The metaphysical essence of representation is stated in an abridged and thus easily misunderstood version in a sentence in a letter of July 11, 1706, to des Bosses (Gerh. II, 311): *"Cum perceptio nihil aliud sit, quam multorum in uno expressio, necesse est omnes Entelechias seu Monades perceptione praeditas esse, neque ulla naturae Machina sua Entelechia propria caret."*[9] The *perceptio* is an essential expression of the monad. It helps to constitute the monad's unity as the beingness of beings. It has its own essence in "expressing a manifold in unity." The *expressio* is a presenting unfolding, a *développer* (Gerh. IV, 523), which belongs to the gathering enfolding, *envelopper,* and is understood expressly as *représenter.* The "perceptions" are *"les représentations du composé, ou de ce qui est dehors, dans le simple"* (*Principes de la Nature et de la Grace, fondés en raison,* Gerh. VI, 598).[10] The *unum* in which the *multa* are unfolded, that is, explicated and presented in a collected manner, is the "simple." The simple, unifying of itself,

8. "The passing condition which involves and represents a multiplicity in the unity, or in the simple substance, is nothing else than what is called Perception. This should be carefully distinguished from Apperception or Consciousness . . ."

9. "Since perception is nothing else than the expression of many in one, it is necessary that all entelechies, or monads, be provided with perception. No natural machine lacks its own entelechy."

10. "Representations of the compound, or of what is external, in the simple."

presents the manifold to itself, and has the essence of its self-containedness, its constancy, that is, its reality in this presenting representation itself. **1773866**

Leibniz does not understand the Aristotelian word *entelecheia* in a Greek manner, but rather in the sense of his monadologic thinking: *"On pourrait donner le nom d'*Entéléchies *à toutes les substances simples ou Monades créées, car elles ont en elles une certaine perfection (echousi to enteles), il y a une suffisance (autarkeia) qui les rend sources de leurs actions internes et pour ainsi dire des Automates incorporels."*[11] (*Monadologie* paragraph 18, cf. paragraph 48.) In accordance with its "persistent" activity of unifying, the monad has a certain completeness working within itself which constitutes its *actualitas* (reality). "True unity," that is, the substantiality of substance, is contained in the essence of this reality as simple, unifying, representing effectuation. *". . . Dico substantiam . . . esse una Entelechia actuatam, sine qua nullum esset in ea principium verae Unitatis."*[12] In contrast, the unity of those *entia*, which are such *entia per aggregationem*, is a unity *"a cogitatione; idemque est in quovis aggregato, ut nihil vere unum invenias, si Entelechiam demas."*[13] (Letter of June 20, 1703, to de Volder, Gerh. II, 250.)

However, what the unifying representation unfolds and presents to representation is no arbitrary *multum*, but rather a definitely limited manifold in which the universe is mirrored. The manifold is in each case the world, *mundus*, but representing itself according to the *modus spectandi*, in which the *perceptio* of the monad is held. In accordance with this manner of seeing and its point of

11. "The name of *entelechies* might be given to all simple substances or created monads, for they have within themselves a certain perfection (echousi to enteles); there is a certain sufficiency (autarkeia) which makes them the sources of their internal activities, and so to speak, incorporeal automata."

12. "I say that a substance is actuated by one entelechus without which it would contain no principle of true unity."

13. "Whose unity comes from thought. This is the same in every aggregate; you will find no true unity if you take away the entelechy."

view, the world is concentrated in such a way that the universe mirrors itself in effecting unifying representation, and every monad itself can be addressed as a living mirror of the universe, effecting of itself.

In the fifth letter to Clarke, Leibniz says with great conciseness: *"chaque substance simple en vertu de sa nature est, pour dire ainsi, une concentration et un miroir vivant de tout l'univers suivant son point de vue."*[14] (Gerh. VII, 411, n. 87.) Because every being is determined as monad in its reality by simple unifying effectuation in the sense of representation from its point of view, the monads ("entelechies") are necessarily of themselves different from each other: *"Entelechias differre necesse est, seu non esse penitus similes inter se, imo principia esse diversitatis, nam aliae aliter exprimunt universum ad suum quaeque spectandi modum, idque ipsarum officium est ut sint totidem specula vitalia rerum seu totidem Mundi concentrati."*[15] (Letter of June 20, 1703, to de Volder, Gerh. II, 251/52.) The unfolding-gathering essence of the *perceptio* is thus first revealed in the simple originality of "world formation" and in mirroring effecting itself.

But this, too, only hints at the essential realm of the *perceptio*, although in such a way that its fundamental characteristic as effecting *(actio)* first becomes evident, and the essential core of the *actualitas* is determined. Representation—presenting the universe from a point of view and representing it only in a concentration corresponding to the point of view and thus never attaining what is truly sought after—is in itself transitional in that it is essentially together with its actual world and drives beyond that world through its relation to the universe. A progression driving beyond itself is thus active in representation: *principium mutationis "est inter-*

14. "Every simple substance is by its nature (if one may say so) a concentration and a living mirror of the whole universe, according to its point of view."

15. "Entelechies must necessarily differ or not be completely similar to each other; in fact, they are principles of diversity, for they each express the universe from their own point of view. This is their office, that they should be so many living mirrors or so many concentrated worlds."

num omnibus substantiis simplicibus, . . . consistitque in progressu percep-
tionum Monadis cuiusque, nec quicquam ultra habet tota rerum natura. "[16]
(Letter of June 30, 1704, to de Volder, Gerh. II, 271.)

In accordance with its own essence, representation is transitional in that it drives toward transition. This striving is the fundamental characteristic of effecting in the sense of representing. *"L'ac-*
tion du principe interne, qui fait le changement ou le passage d'une
perception à une autre, peut être appelé Appétition; *il est vrai, que l'appétit*
ne saurait toujours parvenir entièrement à toute la perception où il tend,
mais il en obtient toujours quelque chose, et parvient à des perceptions
nouvelles."[17] (*Monadologie,* section 15, Gerh. VI, 609.) The striving
(appetitus) in which the monad effects its own unity for itself is, on
the other hand, essential representing in itself. The simple self-
containedness of what is truly persistent (*persistens,* to de Volder,
January 21, 1704, Gerh. II, 262) consists in representing as striving.
Perceptio and *appetitus* are not two determinations of the reality of
what is real which are first produced. Rather their essential unity
constitutes the simplicity of what is truly one, and thus its unity and
its beingness. *"Imo rem accurate considerando dicendum est nihil in rebus*
esse nisi substantias simplices et in his perceptionem atque appetitum" (Letter of June 30, 1704, to de Volder, Gerh. II, 270).[18]

The simple unifying unity is originally effecting in accordance
with the manner of representational striving. This originally effecting unity is the point of departure for everything transitional and
transitory in beings, from which stems the relation to the one totality of the All. This relation rules in all occurrences in advance. This

16. "The principle of change is internal to all simple substances, . . . and it
consists in the progress of the perceptions of each monad, the entire nature of things
containing nothing besides."
17. "The action of the internal principle, which causes the change of the passage
from one perception to another, may be called *appetition;* it is true that desire cannot
always completely attain to the whole perception to which it tends, but it always
attains something of it and reaches new perceptions."
18. "Indeed, considering the matter carefully, it may be said that there is nothing
in the world except simple substances and, in them, perception and appetite."

unity is *principium internum*. Leibniz calls the principle of beings as such: *vis, la force,* force. The essence of force is not determined by the retroactive generalization of something effecting which we experience somewhere, but the other way around: the essence of force is the original essence of the beingness of beings.

What truly is shows itself in the light of the truth which has become certainty, as the *cogitare* of the *ego cogito*. The essence of force is defined in reflection upon the Being of what truly is. It is only from this essence of force that individual forces receive the character of their dependent (derivative) essence. The first version of section 12 of the *Monadology* says this clearly: *"Et généralement on peut dire que la force n'est autre chose que le principe du changement."*[19] "Change" does not mean here any kind of becoming-different in general, but rather the transitional essence of striving representation in accordance with whose manner every being *is,* insofar as it is. Force, the fundamental characteristic of simple unifying unity, is thus also adequately called *vis primitiva activa* because it rules pure effecting in its essence in a simple and original way. It is the *subiectum* and the basis (*Monadologie,* section 48), the underlying supporting constant in whose effecting the constancy of beings have their closest origination, although not a radically producing origination (*originatio radicalis*).

Every *subiectum* is determined in its *esse* by *vis (perceptio—appetitus)*. Every *substantia* is monad. Thus the essence of the reality of the *res cogitans* developing in the light of truth as certainty attains its scope in which it rules everything real. Together with the universality of the representational essence of reality, the fundamental characteristic of representing, striving, reveals itself so that unity as the essence of beingness first gains its full character from the essence of *vis.* Thus the new essence of reality begins to permeate everywhere and explicitly the totality of beings. In such a manner,

19. "And one can say generally that force is nothing other than the principle of change."

the beginning of that metaphysics develops which will remain the ground of history of the modern period.

At the same time, however, what is effecting in such a way (monadically) retains that characteristic of reality which distinguishes the *actualitas* as *causalitas.* The *causa prima* is the *suprema substantia.* But its effecting also changes in accordance with the essential change of reality. As essential production in the sense of representational striving, the effecting of the original unity, *"Unité primitive,"* (*Monadologie* section 47) emanates to the individual real being which has its limitation in the manner of its point of view. In accordance with that range of view (perspective), the capability is determined of mirroring the universe in such and such a manner, that is, of allowing it to shine. For this reason, the created substances, too, originate so to speak *"par des Fulgurations continuelles de la Divinité de moment à moment"* (*Monadologie,* section 47).[20] In this continual fulguration from moment to moment of the divinity of the god, sparks originate striving toward light, and correspondingly let the light of the divinity continue to shine, and copy it. Everything real is monadical in its reality: not, however, in the same way, but in gradations. Thus Leibniz can say: *"Meae enuntiationes universales esse solent, et servare analogiam."*[21] (Letter of July 11, 1706, to des Bosses, Gerh. II, 311.)

Leibniz's thinking stands under the necessity of the essence of Being thus revealed, which produces what is real in its actual reality in the simplicity of representing and striving unification and thus suffices for the essence of the constancy of what is self-contained. *"Facile enim vides simplices substantias nihil aliud esse posse quam fontes seu principia [simul et subjecta] totidem perceptionis serierum sese ordine evolventium . . . quibus suam perfectionem quantum fas fuit suprema substantia in substantias multas ab ipsa pendentes diffudit, quas singulas tanquam concentrationes universi et (alias prae aliis) tanquam divinitatis*

---

20. "by continual fulgurations of the Divinity from moment to moment."
21. "My propositions are usually universal and retain analogy."

imitamenta concipere oportet. " (Undated letter to de Volder, Gerh. II, 278.)[22]

Striving and representational effecting is the essence of the *esse* of every *subiectum.* This essence constitutes the fundamental character of *existentia.* In accordance with the essence of truth which, having become certainty, requires Being as representing self-production, a being, if it is going to exist at all, must exist in this way insofar as it exists. *"Neque alias rerum rationes puto intelligi et (summatim) vel optari posse, et vel nullo vel hoc modo res existere debuisse."* (1.c.)[23]

But since the beginning of metaphysics, the *existentia* which then first came to essence has had precedence over the *essentia* in that the essential character of reality determines that of possibility. This does not exclude the fact that, in reverse, what is possible previously determines what is correspondingly real. In the beginning of metaphysics, the *prote* and the *deutera ousia* still develop from the essence of presence which is not explicitly grounded. Soon they let this origin become completely forgotten, particularly in the transition from *energeia* to *actualitas.* Thus *potentia* and *actus* appear as two manners of Being which is not determined more precisely. The *necessitas* joins these two in subsequent metaphysics as the third modality.

The new essential appearance of reality in the beginning of modern metaphysics brings along the related change of the *potentia,* so that the distinction of *essentia* and *existentia* changes as a distinction, too, until it is completely reabsorbed in the presencing of

22. "You can easily see that simple substances can be nothing else than just as many sources or principles [and also subjects] of perception of series disclosing themselves in order . . . by which the supreme substance scattered its perfection, as much as possible, into many substances depending upon itself, which substances are to be conceived of individually as concentrations of the universe and as imitations (some more than others) of divinity."

23. "I think that no other reasons for things could be understood or (in brief) desired: A thing ought to exist in this or no other way."

Being itself with the renewed essential character of reality as something essentially unconditional.

It is only from the change of the nature of the *existentia* already accomplished that Leibniz's short treatise "De primae philosophiae Emendatione, et de Notione Substantiae" (1694; Gerh. IV, 468 ff.) receives its true import right down to the title. Looking back to the traditional distinction of *potentia* and *actus*, the *vis* is characterized, so to speak, as the intermediate being between the two. In truth, this signifies overcoming the previous concepts of possibility and reality. The inquiry, however, is in the service of the improvement of "first philosophy" which asks about the beingness of beings and acknowledges the *substantia* as what truly is. *Vis* is the name for the Being of self-contained beings. Accordingly, this Being consists neither in the *actualitas*, in that it means the production of what merely lies present, nor in the *potentia* in the sense of the predisposition of a thing for something (for example, of the tree trunk for a wooden beam). The *vis* has the character of *conatus*, of the already driving endeavor of a possibility. The *conatus* is in itself *nisus*, the inclination to realization. *Tendentia* thus belongs to *vis*, and signifies the striving to which representational thinking belongs. Endeavoring, inclined self-exerting production is the fundamental trait of the constancy in virtue of which actual beings bring themselves about, that is, develop to a *mundus concentratus*. Representing, striving stabilization is the nature of *existentia*. The modalities "possibility" and "necessity" are *modi existendi*.

The nature of the *existentia* which is expressed for the first time shows its authoritative emanation throughout all the fundamental characteristics of beingness and its corresponding basic principle "of the ground" in twenty-four short sections which Leibniz once wrote down. The hidden succinctness and cogency of these sentences, seemingly just following each other, first gives us a glimpse of the simplicity of Being which here claims the thinking of a thinker. The "treatise" (Gerh. VII, 289–291), still undated, has no title. We shall call it "The Twenty-four Statements" (cf. pp. 49–54).

Of course they cannot replace the ninety sections of the *Monadology* which are similarly constructed. But Leibniz's thinking really first attains the culmination of its mysterious transparency in these "twenty-four statements." Instead of a thorough interpretation of the "twenty-four statements" which would have to indicate the crux of the implied history of Being, it will be sufficient to mention what directly concerns *the nature of the* existentia.

Being in the sense of the *hoti estin* says that something *is*, and that there is not rather nothing. Thatness *(existentia)* is revealed as the insurrection against nothingness *(ex-sistere ex nihilo)* in that nothingness means absolutely nonexistent. However, as soon as Being enters the essence of effecting, and beingness actually means reality, something like a procedure and an effort, an action of the *actus* is implanted in every being *(res, thing, chose)* as an effected being. Because nothing is needed for it and because every arrangement is superfluous, nothingness is simpler and easier than the real being thus effected. *"Car le rien est plus simple et plus facile que quelque chose."*[24] (*Principes de la Nature et de la Grâce, fondés en raison,* n. 7; Gerh. VI, 602.) But in that beings are, and Nothingness has already made itself known anyhow as what is easier and simpler, the question must be asked: *"Pourquoi il y a plutôt quelque chose que rien?"*[25] (l.c.) This question about the "why" is, of course, only necessary and justified if everything, and thus also the precedence of what is less simple and easy (that is, beings), has its "therefore," that is, its ground before nothingness. The question is supported by the "grand principle" of "metaphysics" which says: *"que rien ne se fait sans raison suffisante."*[26] (l.c.)

But if this "principle" names the essential beginning of what somehow relinquishes nothingness, the *principium grande* must eminently characterize the insurrection against nothingness, and thus

---

24. "For nothing is simpler and easier than something."
25. "Why is there something rather than nothing?"
26. "Nothing happens without a sufficient reason."

the *existentia* itself in its nature. Every being is groundlike: ground-like ground: *hypokeimenon, subiectum.* Being as reality is a grounding. Grounding must contain the nature of giving Being precedence over nothingness. Being must contain the character of being attracted to itself and capable of itself in its essence. Being is unifying self-effecting in self-containedness. It is the striving after itself which brings itself before itself (represents). As Being, the possibility of something possible is already an "existing," that is, essentially related to *existentia.* The possible being is already—because it only "is" at all what it is to that extent—something attracted, an inclined endeavor and thus a grounding and effecting. Being possible (possibility), which is thought and can only be thought from the essence of Being, summons forth in itself representational striving in such a way that this summons already brings about and accomplishes the *existentia.* *"Itaque dici potest* Omne possibile E x i s t i t u r i r e."[27] (The Twenty-four Statements," n. 6.)

The expression *existiturire*, which because of the essentiality of its saying is actually "beautiful" in spite of its seeming misshapenness, is according to the grammatical form a *verbum desiderativum.* The striving of self-effecting, of the *conatus ad Existentiam* (n. 5), is named there. The existential character of possibility is expressed. Existence itself has such a nature that it summons forth the attraction of itself. Thus possibility does not repulse reality, but contains it, retains it in itself, and so remains precisely in possession of its essence whose fundamental trait is *appetitus.* Hence the first of "The Twenty-four Statements" can begin with the sentence: "Ratio *est in Natura, cur aliquid potius existat quam nihil.* " "A ground is in the nature of beings as beings, a reason why something, that is, preferentially and more attractedly, exists rather than nothing." This says: beings in their Being are *exigent* with respect to themselves. "To exist" means in itself: attraction and unifying capability which is an effecting. In that something *is* it is also essentially *potius.*

27. "Thus every possible can be said to strive to exist."

Being as existence in the sense of representational striving which simply and unifyingly effects a *mundus concentratus* (the monad) as *speculum universi* is the new nature of *actualitas.* The prevalence of *existentia* over *nonexistentia* belongs to it. But the essential structure of Being which thus comes to light would not be metaphysical, which it is, if the *causalitas* which has ruled Being since Plato's *agathon* were not still determinative in the nature of *actualitas* as *vis primitiva activa. The metaphysical basic characteristic of the monadic nature of Being appears in the progression of the first four statements:*

The ratio *(cur aliquid potius existat quam nihil) "debet esse in aliquo Ente Reali seu causa"*[28] (n. 2). In contradistinction to the *ens mentale (ideale)*, the *ens reale* is for Leibniz in each case a *res actu existens.* The *ens reale*, which underlies all *rationes* as their *causa, "hoc autem Ens oportet necessarium esse, alioqui causa rursus extra ipsum quaerenda esset cur ipsum existat potius quam non existat, contra Hypothesin. Est scilicet Ens illud ultima ratio Rerum, et uno vocabulo solet appellari* DEUS"[29] (n. 3).

The god who acts here as ground is not thought theologically, but purely ontologically, namely as the highest being in whom all beings and Being itself are caused. However, because Leibniz thinks every manner of Being as *modus existendi* in virtue of the monadically determined *existentia*, the *ens possibile* is not only thought as *existituriens*, but the *ens necessarium* is also thought as *existentificans.*

The fourth statement: *"Est ergo causa cur Existentia praevaleat non-Existentiae, seu* Ens necessarium *est* EXISTENTIFICANS."[30] With

28. "The ground (why something exists rather than nothing) 'ought to be in some real being or cause'. "

29. "But this being must be necessary; otherwise, a ground would again have to be sought why it exists rather than not—contrary to our hypothesis. That being is, of course, the ultimate ground of things and is usually designated by the one word GOD."

30. "Therefore there is a cause why existence prevails over nonexistence, that is, necessary being is that which causes to exist."

this determination of the *facere,* Being's character of production appears in the sense that Being itself is made and effected by a being.

But within the causal nature of beingness permeating metaphysics everywhere in the most various forms, the exigent nature of Being still becomes determinative in the developed beginning of modern metaphysics. The eminence of the *exigere,* however, does not relinquish the representational character of Being; for this character preserves the tradition of the beginning and primal essence of Being which becomes evident as presencing. But now presence has come to be in the *repraesentatio* in virtue of *ousia* and presence through the *veritas* as *certitudo.* However, this presence would be thought too one-sidedly if it were equated with presence in the sense of the representation of what is represented for representing.

The essence of *repraesentatio,* and thus of Being in the sense of *vis* and *existentia,* now enters a peculiar ambiguity. In that it appropriates a world as a perspective of the universe, every monad is originally mirroring from its point of view. In that the monad is representative in such a way, it portrays itself and represents itself, presents itself and thus represents what it requires in its striving. It is what it represents in this manner.

To represent something does not just say: to bring something to oneself, but also: to portray something, namely the representing meant in the first instance. A man "represents something" means: he *is* somebody. This Being belongs to *vis.* As *vis* and *existentia,* Being is at the same time this "representing something," which in turn is always variously brought in the individual monads by these monads themselves to themselves, but first of all and as a whole in the *omnipraesentia* of the highest substance as the central monad. What is everywhere essential is the fact that "presence" is explicitly related back to a kind of ego, and is really accomplished by that ego as its own essential activity. In contradistinction to this representative presence, the presence whose name is *ousia* is a presencing to and from unconcealment, whereby unconcealment is experienced, but no longer itself grounded in its essence.

Correspondingly, *noein* is to be thought as representing only with caution, namely when it has its essential weight in dwelling in unconcealment and when this dwelling, attentive to unconcealment, perceives it. Bringing to itself what is encountered in the safety of what is presented is something quite different from dwelling in unconcealment. *Noein* and *percipere* name essentially different kinds of representation. For Being, which already predetermines what can be represented, is in the first instance *hypokeimenon*, and in the second instance objectivity which is grounded in a *subiectum*, but in a *subiectum* whose essence is not identical with that of *hypokeimenon*.

Subiectity and Subjectivity

In its developed beginning, modern metaphysics brings the essence of Being as reality in the manner of the history of Being to an essential plurality which from then on can never be enunciated in a unified way, and is thus always distorted in some respect by retroactive terms. But perhaps precisely for this reason the first attempt at a contemplation of the history of Being might make use of such terms, even if this procedure only serves the next task of for once preparing for the event that the recollection in this history, nearest to us in time, of the self-contained multiplicity of Being's essence must come to meet us.

The term serving such an intention may be called *subiectity*. The common name subjectivity immediately and all too stubbornly burdens thinking with erroneous opinions which interpret every relation of Being to man, or even to his egoness, as a destruction of objective Being, as if objectivity in all its essential traits did not have to remain caught in subjectivity.

The name subiectity should emphasize the fact that Being is determined in terms of the subiectum, *but not necessarily by an ego.* Moreover, the term contains at the same time a reference to the *hypokeimenon*, and thus to the beginning of metaphysics. It also presages the progression of modern metaphysics which actually does claim egoness, above all the selfhood of the spirit, as an essential characteristic of true reality.

If one understands by subjectivity the idea that the essence of reality is in truth—that is, for the self-certainty of self-consciousness —*mens sive animus, ratio,* reason, spirit, "subjectivity" appears as a manner of subiectity. Subiectity does not necessarily characterize Being in terms of the *actualitas* of representational striving, for subiectity also means that beings are *subiectum* in the sense of *ens actu,* whether this is *actus purus* or *mundus* as *ens creatum.* Subiectity says finally: beings are *subiectum* in the sense of the *hypokeimenon* which has the distinction of being *prote ousia* in the presencing of what is actual.

In its history as metaphysics, Being is through and through subiectity. But where subiectity becomes subjectivity, the *subiectum* preeminent since Descartes, the ego, has a multiple precedence. The ego is on the one hand the truest being, the being most accessible in its certainty. But it is also and as a consequence that being in which we think Being and substance in general, the simple and the composite (*Monadologie,* section 30, Gerh. VI, 612), insofar as we think at all. Finally, spirit, *mens,* has a precedence within the grada- tion of monadic beings. *"Et Mentium maxima habetur ratio, quia per ipsas quam maxima varietas in quam minimo spatio obtinetur."* ("The Twenty-four Statements," n. 21.) In the *mentes,* an eminent repre- senting and striving is possible, and thus the effecting of an eminent presence. *"Et dici potest Mentes esse primarias Mundi unitates"* (n. 22).

However, for the modern history of metaphysics, the name subjectivity expresses the full essence of Being only when Being's character of representation is not thought about simply or even predominantly, but rather when *appetitus* and its developments as a fundamental characteristic of Being have become evident. Ever since the developed beginning of modern metaphysics, Being is will, that is, *exigentia essentiae.* "Will" contains a manifoldness of essence. It is the will of reason or the will of spirit, it is the will of love or the will to power.

Because the will, and thus also the representation active in it, are known as human faculties and activities, it seems as if a thorough humanization of Being had come about. As modern metaphysics and thus all metaphysics comes closer to its completion, anthropomorphism is expressly required and adopted as the truth, although the fundamental position of anthropomorphism is grounded by Schelling and Nietzsche in different ways.

The name subiectity names the unified history of Being, beginning with the essential character of Being as *idea* up to the completion of the modern essence of Being as the will to power. The multiplicity of the modern essence already takes shape in the developed beginning of modern metaphysics:

Being is reality in the sense of indubitable representation.

Being is reality in the sense of representational striving which in each case unifies a being which is a world in terms of simple unity.

As such unification Being is *actualitas*.

However, as effecting (being attracted) reality, Being has the fundamental characteristic of will.

As this willing, Being is the stabilization of constancy which still remains a becoming.

In that every willing is self-willing, Being is eminently characterized by "coming toward itself" whose real essence is attained in reason as selfhood.

Being is the will to will.

All of these characteristics of Being which belong to subiectity as subjectivity develop a unified essence which, in accordance with its *exigent* character, develops itself and thus the whole of beings in its own unity, that is, in the conformation of its essential structure. When Being has attained the essence of will, it is in itself systematic and a system.

The system, thought as the unity of order of knowledge, appears at first to be merely the paradigm of portrayal for everything knowable in its structure. But because Being as reality is itself will, and will is the unification of the unity of totality striving for itself, the system is no mere schematic order which the thinker has in mind and always presents only incompletely and each time somehow onesidedly. The system, the *Sustasis*, is the essential structure of the reality of what is real—of course, only when reality has been discovered in its essence as will. This happens when truth has become certainty, evoking from the essence of Being the fundamental characteristic of the universal ensurance of structure in a ground which ensures itself.

Because *veritas* does not yet ground its essence in the *certitudo* of the *cogitare* in the medieval period, Being can never be systematic. What is called a medieval system is always just a *summa* as the presentation of the whole of doctrine. But the idea of a system is still less commensurate with the philosophy of Plato and Aristotle. The systematic essence of subjectivity first brings the trend toward the unconditionality of manipulation and positing. Here the essence of condition appears as a new form of the causality of beingness, so that reality is true reality only when it has determined in advance of everything real all that is in terms of the systematics of the conditioning unconditioned.

Leibniz, "The Twenty-four Statements"[31]

1. *Ratio* est in Natura, cur aliquid potius existat quam nihil. Id consequens est magni illius principii, quod nihil fiat sine ratione, quemadmodum etiam cur hoc potius existat quam aliud rationem esse oportet.

2. Ea ratio debet esse in aliquo Ente Reali seu causa. Nihil aliud enim *causa* est, quam realis ratio, neque veritates possibilitatum et *necessitatum* (seu negatarum in opposito possibilitatum) aliquid efficerent nisi possibilitates fundarentur in re actu existente.

---

31. 1. There is a *ground* in nature why something exists rather than nothing. This is a consequence of the great principle that nothing exists without a ground, just as there also must be a ground why this exists rather than something else.

3. Hoc autem Ens oportet necessarium esse, alioqui causa rursus extra ipsum quaerenda esset cur ipsum existat potius quam non existat, contra Hypothesin. Est scilicet Ens illud ultima ratio Rerum, et uno vocabulo solet appellari DEUS.

4. Est ergo causa cur Existentia praevaleat non-Existentiae, seu *Ens necessarium* est Existentificans.

5. Sed quae causa facit ut aliquid existat, seu ut possibilitas exigat existentiam, facit etiam ut omne possibile habeat conatum ad Existentiam, cum ratio restrictionis ad certa possibilia in universali reperiri non possit.

6. Itaque dici potest *Omne possibile* Existiturire, prout scilicet fundatur in Ente necessario actu existente, sine quo nulla est via qua possibile perveniret ad actum.

7. Verum hinc non sequitur omnia possibilia existere: sequeretur sane si omnia possibilia essent compossibilia.

---

2. This ground ought to be in some real being or cause. For a *cause* is nothing else than a real ground, and the truths of possibilities and *necessities* (or negativities in the opposition of possibilities) would not produce anything unless the possibilities were grounded in an actually existing thing.

3. But this being must be necessary; otherwise, a ground would again have to be sought why it exists rather than not—contrary to our hypothesis. That being is, of course, the ultimate ground of things and is usually designated by the one word GOD.

4. Therefore there is a cause why existence prevails over nonexistence, that is, *necessary being* is that which causes to exist *(existentificans)*.

5. But this cause which makes something to exist, or some possibility to demand existence, also makes every possible to have a striving for existence, since, in general, a reason for restricting to only some possibles cannot be found.

6. Thus *every possible* can be said to strive to exist *(existiturire)* according as it is grounded in a necessary being actually existing, without which there is no way for a possible to become actual.

7. Still it does not follow from this that all possibles exist. It would follow, by all means, if all possibles were compossible.

8. Sed quia alia aliis incompatibilia sunt, sequitur quaedam possibilia non pervenire ad existendum, suntque alia aliis incompatibilia, non tantum respectu ejusdem temporis, sed et in universum, quia in praesentibus futura involvuntur.

9. Interim ex conflictu omnium possibilium existentiam exigentium hoc saltem sequitur, ut Existat ea rerum series, per quam plurimum existit, seu series omnium possibilium maxima.

10. Haec etiam series sola est determinata, ut ex lineis recta, ex angulis rectus, ex figuris maxime capax, nempe circulus vel sphaera. Et uti videmus liquida sponte naturae colligi in guttas sphaericas, ita in natura universi series maxima capax existit.

11. Existit ergo perfectissimum, cum nihil aliud *perfectio* [missing in Gerhardt] sit quam quantitas realitatis.

12. Porro perfectio non in sola materia collocanda est, seu in replente tempus et spatium, cujus quocunque modo eadem fuisset quantitas, sed in forma seu varietate.

---

8. But because some possibles are incompatible with others, it follows that certain possibles do not attain existence. Moreover, some possibles are incompatible with others not only in regard to occurring at the same time, but also, in general, because future possibles are involved in present ones.

9. Nevertheless, from the conflict of all the possibles demanding existence, this at least follows, that there exists that series of things by which the maximum could exist, that is, the maximal series of all possibles.

10. Only this series is determined, so that of lines straight ones are determinate; of angles, a right one; of figures, one with greatest capacity, to be sure, a circle or a sphere. And as we see liquids collect according to the will of nature in spherical drops, so in the nature of the universe the series of maximal capacity came to be.

11. Therefore the most perfect came to be since *perfection* [missing in Gerhardt] is nothing else than quantity of reality.

12. However, perfection is not to be placed in matter alone, that is, in filling time and space, whose quantity would be in whatever way the same, but in form or variety.

13. Unde jam consequitur materiam non ubique similem esse, sed per formas reddi dissimilarem, alioqui non tantum obtineretur varietatis quantum posset. Ut taceam quod alibi demonstravi, nulla alioqui diversa phaenomena esse extitura.

14. Sequitur etiam eam praevaluisse seriem, per quam plurimum oriretur distinctae cogitabilitatis.

15. Porro distincta cogitabilitas dat ordinem rei et pulchritudinem cogitanti. Est enim *ordo* nihil aliud quam relatio plurium distinctiva. Et confusio est, cum plura quidem adsunt, sed non est ratio quodvis a quovis distinguendi.

16. Hinc tolluntur atomi, et in universum corpora, in quibus nulla est ratio quamvis partem distinguendi a quavis.

17. Sequiturque in universum, Mundum esse *kosmon*, plenum ornatus, seu ita factum ut maxime satisfaciat intelligenti.

18. *Voluptas* enim intelligentis nihil aliud est quam perceptio pulchritudinis, ordinis, perfectionis. Et omnis dolor continet aliquid inordinati sed respective ad percipientem, cum absolute omnia sint ordinata.

---

13. Whence it follows that matter is not everywhere uniform, but becomes diversified through forms; otherwise, not as much variety as possible would obtain. To pass over in silence what I have demonstrated elsewhere—no diverse phenomena would otherwise appear.

14. It follows also that that series prevailed by which there emerges the greatest possibility of thinking of things as distinct.

15. Further, the possibility of thinking of things as distinct gives order to the thing and beauty to the thinker. For *order* is nothing but the distinctive relation between many things, and confusion arises when there are many things, but no ground for distinguishing anything from anything else.

16. Hence atoms are done away with and, in general, bodies in which there is no ground for distinguishing any part from any other.

17. And it follows, in general, that the world is a *cosmos*, fully adorned, that is, so made as to give the most satisfaction to the perceiver.

18. For the *pleasure* of the perceiver is nothing but the perception of beauty,

19. Itaque cum nobis aliqua displicet in serie rerum, id oritur ex defectu intellectionis. Neque enim possibile est ut omnis Mens omnia distincte intelligat, et partes tantum alias prae aliis observantibus, non potest apparere Harmonia in toto.

20. Ex his consequens est, in Universo etiam justitiam observari, cum *Justitia* nihil aliud sit quam ordo seu perfectio circa Mentes.

21. Et Mentium maxima habetur ratio, quia per ipsas quam maxima varietas in quam minimo spatio obtinetur.

22. Et dici potest Mentes esse primarias Mundi unitates, proximaque simulacra entis primi, quia rationes distincte percipiunt necessarias veritates, id est rationes quae movere Ens primum et universum formare debuerunt.

23. Prima etiam causa summae est *Bonitatis,* nam dum quantum plurimum perfectionis producit in rebus, simul etiam quantum plurimum voluptatis mentibus largitur, cum *voluptas* consistat in perceptione perfectionis (instead of: perceptionis).

---

order, perfection. And every pain contains something of disorder, but only with respect to the perceiver, since absolutely all things are ordered.

19. And so when something dissatisfies us in the series of things, it arises from a defect in the intellect. It is impossible for every mind to understand all things distinctly, and the harmony of the whole cannot be seen by those who observe only some parts rather than others.

20. It is a consequence of this that justice is observed in the universe, since *justice* is nothing but the order or perfection that obtains in respect to minds.

21. And the greatest ground belongs to minds, because through them is obtained as much variety in as little space as possible.

22. And it can be said that minds are the primary unities of the world and the closest images of prime being, because they perceive grounds distinctly as necessary truths, that is, grounds which were bound to move prime being and to form the universe.

23. The first cause is of the highest *goodness,* for, while it produces as much perfection as possible in things, it also bestows as much pleasure as possible

24. Usque adeo ut mala ipsa serviant ad majus bonum, et quod dolores reperiuntur in Mentibus, necesse sit proficere ad majores voluptates.

(N. 11 and n. 23 are corrected following the manuscript.)

---

on minds, since *pleasure* consists in the perception of perfection (instead of: perception).

24. In order that evils themselves may serve the greater good, and because disappointments are found in minds, it is necessary to advance to higher pleasures.

TWO

Sketches for a History of Being as Metaphysics

FROM THE HISTORY OF BEING

1. *Aletheia*, barely presencing and not returning to the origin, but rather going forth to mere unconcealedness, comes under the yoke of the *idea*.

2. Viewed from the *arche*, the subjugation of *aletheia* stems from a release of beings to presence thus beginning.

3. The subjugation of *aletheia* is the preeminence of appearing and showing itself of the *idea;* the *hen* as *phainotaton*.

4. The precedence of the *idea* brings the *ti estin* along with the *eidos* to the position of authoritative Being. Being is primarily whatness.

We must consider how whatness as *exclusive Being (idea* as *ontos on)* gives more room to being itself, the *on* nominally conceived, than to the *on* verbally conceived. The undecidedness of beings and Being in the *on*, and its ambiguity.

5. The precedence of whatness brings the precedence of beings themselves in what they are. The precedence of beings establishes Being as *koinon* in terms of the *hen*. The eminent character of metaphysics is decided. The one as unifying unity becomes authoritative for subsequent determination of Being.

6. As authoritative Being, whatness usurps the realm of Being, namely Being in the primal determination lying *before* the distinc-

tion of what and that, which preserves for Being the fundamental characteristic of originating and emerging and presencing, thus of that which subsequently appears as thatness *(hoti estin)*, but first and only in contrast to the precedence of whatness *(idea)*. Thus the *prote ousia* determined by Aristotle is precisely no longer the primal presencing of Being. Accordingly, the later *existentia* and existence can never reach back to the original essential fullness of Being, not even when it is thought in its Greek origin.

We must consider how the that of the *existentia* never again attains the *esti (eon) gar einai.*

7. The ambiguity of the *eon* and *on*, not thought grammatically. What the nominal (beings themselves) and the verbal (Being) means when thought primally.

How the ambiguity of the *on* includes the distinction.

8. The transformation of Being to certainty stems from the criterion of whatness.

9. The essence of thatness (reality) which remains taken for granted in its essential character finally permits the equation of unconditional certainty with absolute reality.

10. All events in the history of Being which is metaphysics have their beginning and ground in the fact that metaphysics leaves and must leave the essence of Being undecided, in that it remains indifferent from the beginning to a regarding of what is worthy of question in favor of saving its own essence, and indeed in the indifference of not-knowing.

Toward an Essential Determination of Modern Metaphysics

1. In the essential change of truth as *veritas* to *certitudo*, Being is prefigured as the representedness of self-representing in which the essence of subiectity develops. The simplest name for the determination of the beingness of beings in preparation here is the will, *will as willing-itself.*

The essential fullness of the will cannot be determined with respect to the will as a faculty of the soul. The will must rather be brought to essential unity with appearance: *idea, re-praesentatio,* becoming evident, portraying *itself,* attaining *itself,* transcending *itself,* and thus "having *itself,*" and thus "being."

2. The necessity of the system as the constitution of subiectity, that is, of Being as the beingness of beings, lies in the essential constituents of the will understood in this way.

3. The system is a system only as an absolute system.

4. Hence the two characteristics of modern metaphysics' essential completion: (1) the manner in which the concept of philosophy is determined by the absolute system; (2) the manner in which the system is distorted and negated in the most extreme completion of metaphysics by Nietzsche.

OBJECTIVITY—TRANSCENDENCE—UNITY—BEING
(*Critique of Pure Reason,* section 16)

The system:

Unity—*ousia*—*hen* as unity of "standing together" before consciousness and for consciousness.

Standing together determines the essence of unity.

However, unity itself must be determined and questioned in its essence in the question about the truth of Being.

Co-agito, legein, gathering: *Hen* and *Logos.*

Together: collected—present.

Standing: constancy.

Representation and letting stand together.

Representation as "certain," *certum,* as securing.

Certainty as guarantee of stability. System.

Then what does the Kantian "I think" mean?

Something like: I represent something as something, that is, I let something stand together before me. Unity is necessary for standing together and is in essence determined by it.

Unity is the condition (of synthesis and connection); but its

57

essence is itself conditioned by the essence of "standing together" (section 16): that standing together presences at all, that Being presences as *hen* and not nothing.

Together—*para.*

Stand: place, posit, *ponere; sistere:* Sistence, Position.

Standing-there—*stasis.*

Appearance—*eidos, idea.*

But everything already in the presence, *ousia,* of the *ego cogito cogitationes.*

BEING—OBJECTIVITY (WILL)

Since the fifteenth century, the word, "object" has had the meaning of: opposition.

For Luther, object means:

> the opposed "status":
> the Jewish status and the Christian status:
> "to adopt the opposing status."

Since the eighteenth century, the word has been taken as the translation of *obiectum.* A quarrel begins as to whether one should say ob-ject or ob-stacle.

Ob-ject and representation: *re-praesentare.*

For a carpenter the wood is the object, that is, "what he works against"—when he functions as cause.

With regard to the ontic-ontological distinction of beings and Being, what is objective is that in the object which has color, extension, etc.; what is objective: what constitutes its standing against as such.

BEING AS OBJECTIVITY—BEING AND THINKING— UNITY AND THE HEN

How does objectivity take on the character of constituting the essence of beings as such?

One thinks Being as objectivity, and then tries from there to find beings in themselves. Only one forgets to question and to say what one means by "in being." What "is" Being?

Being—unquestioned and a matter of course and thus unthought and uncomprehended in a truth which has long since been forgotten, and is groundless.

Being is beingness; beingness as *ousia* is presence, continual presence with its space-time forgotten.

Presence grounds the *para*, the "with." The "with" supports and bears the "together" and the "together with"; the latter can, of course, be taken for unity and one, but at the same time remain unperceived and forgotten in its true essence.

Stability grounds constancy together with presence (verbal) as *ob*-jectivity when the "ob" becomes essential through the *re-praesentatio*. When does this happen? With the insurrection of the *subiectum qua ego* as *res cogitans qua certum*. Thus unity comes as the changed form of *ousia*, determined by truth as certainty, to the relation to representational thinking which necessarily looks with regard and *as* regard representing toward unity, and which is the "I connect" in the manner of representation. Primally, however, the *hen* is understood neither in terms of "I think" nor in terms of *idea*, but rather from *nous*(Parmenides) and *logos* in Heraclitus's sense as the gathering that reveals and secures.

OBJECTIVITY AND REFLEXION
REFLEXION AND NEGATIVITY

The question about the essential origin of the "object" in general. That is the question about the truth of beings in modern metaphysics. (Unity and objectivity; essence of unity, *ousia*.)

Hegel's determination of experience as allowing the new true object to originate shows the formulation of the object's concept in the absolute transcendental sense. Hence this is the place for a necessary reflection upon the essence of the object in general. (The misunderstanding of the "theory of the object.")

Object in the sense of ob-ject: Only when man becomes subject, that is, where the subject becomes the ego and the ego becomes the *ego cogito*, only where this *cogitare* is understood in its essence as "original synthetic unity of transcendental apperception," only where the culmination for "logic" is reached (in truth as the certainty of the "I think"), only there is the essence of the object revealed in its objectivity. Only there is it at the same time possible and inevitable to understand this objectivity itself as "the new true object," and to think it as unconditional.

Decisive: Kant—in that doctrine which is unobtrusively contained in a side remark in the *Critique of Pure Reason*; an addition, but filled with essential insight and critical dialogue with Leibniz and all previous metaphysics as Kant himself views it (cf. *Critique of Pure Reason*, "Supplement" to the transcendental analytic: "Of the Amphiboly of the Concepts of Reflection").

"Reflexion," understood in the light of the history of Being, of human being: shining back into *aletheia* without *aletheia* itself being experienced and grounded and coming to "being" *(Wesen)*.

The uncanny element of the shining-back (re-flexion) of what shows itself. Man's settling down in one of his essential places.

Reflexion—certainty, certainty—self-consciousness.

REFLEXION AND REPRESENTATION

Understood in advance as a fundamental characteristic of representational thinking, of the *re-praesentatio*. Reflexion is bending-back, and as such it is the explicitly accomplished presentation of what is present; explicitly, that is, in such a way that what is present is presented to the representer. The bending-back, putting-back, that is, the representation of what is represented which presents *itself* in advance *to itself*, in which what is represented is represented *as* this and that, and is. The "what" itself in its sameness and positedness, constancy.

For this reason reflexion strives for the identical, and for this reason reflexion is a fundamental characteristic of concept formation.

"Concept": What is represented as such, thinking, representing; that is, presenting *itself*. What is represented in the "I think." Thus we must distinguish at first and in general: 1. Reflexion which is already active in the *re-praesentatio* and is not expressed; 2. expressed, explicitly accomplished reflexion. Explicitly accomplished reflexion:

> *a.* As logical (analytic) analysis, comparison (without relation to the object as such): The leaf is green.
>
> *b.* Objective comparison as the connection *(nexus)* of representations among themselves in relation to the object: The sun warms the stone.
>
> *c.* The transcendental condition of the possibility of *b.* When objects are to be judged *a priori*, that is, in a Kantian manner: when something is to be decided upon as to its objectivity, the object is *explicitly* re-presented and presented to the *faculty of representation.* The object as such stands in the unity of intuition and concept. Their unification is the condition of the positing and the constancy of the "over against."

REFLEXION AND OBJECT AND SUBJECTIVITY

Reflexion, object, and subjectivity belong together. Only when reflexion is experienced as such, that is, as the relation to beings, is Being first determinable as objectivity.

The experience of reflexion as this relation presupposes, however, that the relation to beings in general is experienced as *repraesentatio*, as re-presenting, making-present.

This, however, can only become historical (understood in the manner of the history of Being) when *idea* has become idea, that is, *perceptio*. But the change from truth as correspondence to truth as certainty underlies this, the *adaequatio* still being preserved. Certainty as self-ensuring (willing oneself); the *iustitia* as the justification of the relation to beings and their first cause, and thus the belongingness to beings; the *iustitia* in the sense of the reformation and Nietzsche's concept of justice as truth.

Repraesentatio is grounded in *reflexio* in accordance with its essence. Hence the essence of objectivity as such first becomes evident where the essence of thinking is recognized and explicitly enacted as "I think something," that is, as reflexion.

The Transcendental

The transcendental is not the same as the *"a priori,"* but is rather what determines the object as object *a priori*, objectivity. Objectivity is meant in the sense of transcendence. This word then means that something in the object itself goes beyond that object by preceding it, in representing. Transcendence is grounded in "reflexion." Reflexion is transcendental in its true essence, that is, it accomplishes transcendence and thus conditions it in general.

The essential and constant re-servation of thinkability, that is, of the representability of something as the condition of all knowledge. I think something. (Cf. *Critique of Pure Reason*, B XXVI, Preface.)

Repraesentatio and Reflexio

Repraesentatio is grounded in *reflexio*. But *reflexio* is the essence of "thinking," if thinking itself is taken transcendentally as true re-presentation, bringing something as something before oneself, that is, intuition taken in the essential sense. Logic itself is related as transcendental logic to this original re-presentation—presence, presencing, and *ousia*. It is thus meaningless to pit thinking against intuition.

Indeed, the precedence of "intuition," too, is and remains

grounded in the fundamental position of the "I think."

This "intuition" in Kant's sense can never be equated with the precedence of *aletheia*, but only with the precedence of *idea* and the transformation of *aletheia* to *homoiosis* through the precedence of the *idea*, as the germ of development of representing in the sense of making present.

BEING—REALITY—WILL

Being as reality—reality as will.

Will—as self-effectuation striving toward itself in accordance with a re-presentation of itself (the will to will). (All of this presences, shut off from itself, in the opening of Being.)

The will first becomes essential in the *actualitas* where the *ens actu* is determined by the *agere* as *cogitare*, since this *cogito* is *me cogitare*, self-conscious-being, where consciousness as knowingness is essentially presenting-to-oneself. Will as fundamental characteristic of reality.

The volitional basic trait in re-presentation itself as the *perceptio;* hence *perceptio* is in itself *appetitus, co-agitare.*

The will releases itself in truth as certainty. It is brought to the origin by this essence of truth. Will is effecting which plans something according to what is re-presented. Releasing itself in certainty from the misjudgment of the essence of truth; this misjudgment is the deeper unknowing. The will (as essential and fundamental characteristic of beingness) has its essential origin in the intrinsic unknowingness of the essence of truth as the truth of Being. For this reason, metaphysics remains the truth of the Being of beings in the sense of reality as will. This unknowingness, however, rules in the form of the omnicalculation of certainty.

The will has never had the origin as its own. It has always already intrinsically abandoned it by forgetting.

The most profound oblivion is not-recollecting.

BEING AND CONSCIOUSNESS
(Expressed in the Manner of the History of Being)

Consciousness is self-consciousness, and self-consciousness is ego-consciousness or "we"-consciousness.

The essential thing in this is the re-flexive, and in it the "I," "we," "self," the presentation-to-self and self-production.

The will to insure in the overpowering of everything.

The essential thing is "I will myself."

"Consciousness" (as will of the will) must itself now be experienced with regard to the truth of beings (as beingness)—as appropriating of Being. Desolation.

Consciousness is that appropriating in which Being gives itself to truth, that is, leaves truth to beings and beingness, and beingness expropriates truth. The appropriation of expropriation and of directing beings into mere beingness.

REALITY AS WILL
(Kant's Concept of Being)

Will according to Kant: to act in accordance with concepts.

For Kant, Being means:

1. Objectivity—certainty as representedness of experience; in this:
   a. certainty of synthesis
   b. impressionableness of sensibility, both as reality (cf. "The Postulates of All Empirical Thought").
2. Reality of freedom—as thing in itself, that is, will.
3. Cf. 1*b*, impressionableness of sensibility; having an effect— effectiveness.

To consider whether and how these determinations of Being are thought in a unified way, or whether reality (cf. "The Postulates of All Empirical Thought") can from the beginning remain precisely unthought, and how nevertheless ontology can persist as transcendental philosophy.

How the concept of Being of rationalism (*ens certum*—objectivity) and of empiricism (*impressio*—reality) meet in the determination of the reality of what is real. Effectiveness, however, not formal and general, but in the original manner of the history of Being.

Effectiveness and accomplishment: function.

Effectiveness and presence; givenness and impressionability.

Kant's category of "reality" in its essential ambiguity (related to sensibility and thingness at the same time).

Effecting and will, *vis, actus*.

Everywhere the lack of questioning Being.

Most evident in Kant's definition: Being (is) "merely position."

To begin with, the thesis means: Being (is) *merely* the positing of the copula between subject and predicate.

Secondly, the thesis means: Being (in the sense of human being and existence) is the *pure* positing of the thing in departing from its concept.

Finally, the thesis means: Being, the "is" of the copula, aims in the judgment of experience at the positing of the object as a real object (*Critique of Pure Reason*, second edition, section 19).

In the negative form, Kant's thesis about Being as "merely position" means: Being is neither a real predicate with content nor any predicate at all of any thing or object whatever.

Kant's thesis about Being—an ontotheological one, expressed in the context of the question of God's existence in the sense of the *summum ens qua ens realissimum*.

What was without question for Kant is for us worthy of question: the *essential* origin of "*position*" in terms of letting what is present lie present in its presence.

Ponere (posit, place, gather) coming from: thesis, *repraesentatio* (re-presenting), and *legein* (bringing to appear in a revealing way).

BEING

Aletheia (apeiron, logos, hen—arche).
Revealing as the order at the start.

Physis, emergence (going back to itself).
Ousia, presencing, unconcealedness.
Idea, perceivability *(agathon),* causality.
Energeia, workness, assembly, *en-echeia to telos.*
Hypokeimenon, lie present (from *ousia), ergon.*
(Presence—stability—constancy—*aei.)*
Hyparchein, presencing which rules from what already lies present.
Subiectum.
Actualitas: beings—the real—reality
   creator—ens creatum
   causa prima (ens a se).
Certitudo—res cogitans.
Vis—monas (perceptio—appetitus), exigentia essentiae.
Objectivity.
Freedom
   will—representedness
   practical reason.
Will—as absolute knowledge: Hegel.
As will of love: Schelling.
Will to power—eternal recurrence: Nietzsche.
Action and Organization—pragmatism.
The will to will.
Machination (Enframing).

THE COMPLETION OF METAPHYSICS

  The completion of metaphysics sets beings in the abandonment of Being. Being's abandonment of beings is the last reflection of Being as the concealment of unconcealment in which all beings of any sort as such are able to appear. Being's abandonment contains the undecided factor of whether beings persist in their precedence. In the future, this means the question of whether beings undermine and uproot every possibility of the origin in Being, and thus continue to be busy with beings, but also move towards the desolation that does not destroy, but rather chokes what is primal in organizing and ordering. Being's abandonment contains the undecided factor of whether the unconcealment of this concealment, and thus the more primal Origin, is already opening up in this abandonment as an extreme of the concealment of Being. At such a time span of the undecidedness, in which the completion of metaphysics develops and claims human being for the "superman," man seizes upon the rank of what is truly real in itself. The reality of what is real, long since characterized as existence, allots this distinction to man. Man is the truly existent, and existence is determined in terms of human being whose essence has been decided by the beginning of modern metaphysics.

Since thinking, on the edge of the time span of undecidedness in the history of Being, gropes its way toward a first recollection in Being, it must at the same time go through the dominance of human being and leave it aside.

The preeminence of existence in the sense of reality as being-a-self, prefigured in the first completion of metaphysics with Schelling, reaches a peculiar narrowing after being deflected from its way by Kierkegaard, who is neither a theologian nor a metaphysician and yet the essential element of both. The fact that the transformation of reality to the self-certainty of the *ego cogito* is determined directly by Christianity, and the fact that the narrowing of the concept of existence is indirectly determined by Christian factors only proves how Christian faith adopted the fundamental trait of metaphysics and brought metaphysics to Western dominance in this form.

BEING

Effecting, and thus *causalitas* (*agathon*, as what makes possible), lies in "reality" which becomes the dominant basic characteristic of the beingness of beings. Effecting lies in "reality," and effecting contains in itself representation and striving which act in virtue of their own unity. The effecting thus determined is a self-effecting. Herein lies the possible claim of self-ensuring, certainty as self-certainty. Where there is reality, there is will; where there is "will," there is a self-willing; where there is a self-willing, there are possibilities of the essential development of the will as reason, love, power. When and how does the essence of will become essential to reality?

The fact that reality at last enters the essence of will in the completion of metaphysics—and "will" is not to be thought "psychologically," but on the contrary psychology is to be defined by the essence of self-effecting—bears witness to the decisiveness of the essential development of beingness from the pro-gression of Beings to beingness. The primal progression does, however, leave the origin behind as ungrounded, and can therefore place great importance upon organizing itself as pro-gress and going forth.

In the essence of will of beingness as reality, there is concealed machination *(poiesis)*, essentially never accessible to metaphysics, in which *energeia* still has resonance from its primal essential traits in which the progression from the first origin *(aletheia)* takes its decisive beginning which predetermines everything. *Energeia* is, however, at the same time the last preservation of the essence of *physis*, and thus a belonging to the origin.

Existence

What metaphysics generally calls *existentia*, existence, reality, human being is

1. *ousia* of the *hypokeimenon kath'hauto*, that is, of the *hekaston;* the *prote ousia;* presencing as dwelling of what is actual (Aristotle).

2. This *prote ousia* is understood as *energeia* of the *on*, as *tode ti on*, the presencing of what is produced and set up, workness. The broadest name for *einai* as presencing, which at the same time explains its Greek interpretation, is *hyparchein*. There *hypo-keisthai*, what already lies present, is thought together with *arche*, the ruling

origin; *hyparchein* means to rule while already lying present, "ruling forth" thought in a Greek way as to presence of itself.

3. *Energeia* is reinterpreted to mean *actualitas* of the *actus*. *Agere* as *facere, creare*. The pure essence of *actualitas* is the *actus purus* as the *existentia* of the *ens* to whose *essentia existentia* belongs (medieval theology). Accomplishment as effecting what is effected, not allowing to presence in unconcealment, characterizes the *actus*.

4. In accordance with the change of *veritas* to *certitudo*, *actualitas* is understood as *actus* of the *ego cogito*, as *percipere, repraesentare*. The precedence of the *subiectum* in the sense of the ego (Descartes); the *existere* as the *esse* of the *ego sum*; the *repraesentare (percipere)* contrasted with the *noein* as *idein*, and this contrasted with the *noein* of Parmenides. From Being as presence, Being comes to be as representedness in the subject.

5. The *repraesentare* as *perceptio-appetitus* in the sense of the *vis primitiva activa* is the *actualitas* of every *subiectum* in the old sense, and determines the essence of substance as monad. The corresponding distinction of phenomenon and *phainesthai*.

Existentia is now *exigentia essentiae*; its *principium* the *perfectio*, *perfectio* is *gradus essentiae*; *essentia*, however, *nisus ad existendum*.

The Scholastic distinction of *potentia* and *actus*, which itself represents a reinterpretation of the Aristotelian distinction *dynamis-energeia*, is overcome (Leibniz).

6. Existence as *actualitas*, reality, effectedness and effectingness, becomes the objectivity of experience, and thus a modality along with possibility and necessity.

7. The unconditional certainty of the will knowing itself as absolute reality (spirit, love).

Existence as Being is determined from the "real" distinction of the Being of beings according to ground of existence and existence of the ground.

Because the will constitutes the essence of Being, the distinction belongs to willing itself: the will of the ground and the will of reason.

Existence: becoming revealed, bringing oneself to oneself, self-being in self-becoming, against and opposing the ground.

Becoming "contradictory" in itself (Schelling).

8. Existence in Schelling's sense is *narrowed* by Kierkegaard to the being who "is" in the contradiction of temporality and eternity, to man who wills to be himself. Existing as faith, that is, trust in the reality of the real being which man himself is.

Faith as revelation before God. Trust in the reality that God became man.

Faith as being a Christian in the sense of becoming a Christian.

9. Existence in Kierkegaard's sense, only without the essential relation to Christian faith, being a Christian. Being a self as personality in virtue of communication with others. Existence in the relationship to "Transcendence" (K. Jaspers).

10. Existence—sometimes used in *Being and Time* as ecstatic perduring the opening of the there of human being.

Perduring the truth of Being, grounded upon the explicit grounding of the ontological difference, that is, the distinction between beings and Being (outside of all metaphysics and existential philosophy).

11. How the distinction of *essentia* and *existentia* disappears in Nietzsche's metaphysics, why it must disappear in the end of metaphysics, how nevertheless in just this way the greatest distance from the origin is attained.

But disappearance can only be shown by trying to make the distinction visible: will to power as *essentia;* eternal recurrence of the same as *existentia* (cf. "Nietzsche's Metaphysics").

BEING AND THE NARROWING DOWN OF THE CONCEPT OF EXISTENCE

1. The emphatic use of the concept of existence in Schelling's distinction of existence of the ground and ground of existence (Being as will).

2. The restriction of this concept of existence to the faith of

Christians through Kierkegaard (existence—being a Christian) (faith—theology).

3. The adoption of Kierkegaard's concept of existence in "existential philosophy" (K. Jaspers). Existence: being-a-self—communication—metaphysics.

4. Existence as a character of human being in *Being and Time* (History of Being).

Here neither Kierkegaard's concept nor that of existential philosophy is at stake. Rather, existence is thought by returning to the ecstatic character of human being[1] with the intention of interpreting being-open[2] in its eminent relation to the truth of Being. The occasional use of the concept of existence is determined solely by this question. The question serves only to prepare for an overcoming of metaphysics. All this is outside of existential philosophy and existentialism. Thus it is profoundly different from Kierkegaard's passion which is at bottom theological. But it does remain in the essential critical dialogue with metaphysics.

In what sense the concept of the *existentielle* can and must appear with Schelling for the first time.

The existentielle, that is, what exists viewed with reference to its existence, that is, however, *as an existing being;* more precisely, beings, thought in terms of their existing, as *existing beings.*

One must pay attention to the shift in Schelling's terminology here:

> ground—existence
> existence—existing being.

SCHELLING AND KIERKEGAARD

Existence: *being a self*—subjectivity (the will of reason, *ego cogito*)
  revelation
  contradiction————distinction

1. *Dasein.*
2. *Da-sein.*

"passion"—"drive"—"knowing will"—"becoming"
But for Kierkegaard:

1. restricted to man, only *he* exists.
2. Existence—interest in existence, reality.
3. This interest is not a representation, but faith in . . . , committing oneself to what is real, letting oneself be concerned with what is real.
4. Faith in another, not as relation to a doctrine and its truth, but as relation to the true as the real, to concresce with it, concretely.

Existence in the modern sense.

5. Faith that God existed as man, infinitely interested—faith as being a Christian, that is, becoming a Christian.

Lack of faith as *sin.*

SCHELLING

"Willing is primal being."
All Being is the same as existing: existence.
But existence is existence of the ground.
Existence and ground of existence belong to Being.
This distinction belongs to Being as a "real" one.
Being itself is of such a nature that beings as such divide *themselves.*
This distinction lies in the essence of willing.
The distinction: will of the ground and will of reason. How so? The will in willing is reason.
Schelling's "distinction" signifies an opposition (strife) which structures and rules all essence (beings in their beingness), all of this always based upon subjectivity.
Primal being—is will.
Being (not yet being-a-being) closedness.
A being (substantive, verbal-transitive): the self.
being-in-itself.

EXISTENCE AND THE EXISTENTIELLE

The existentielle means this: In his humanity man is not only related to what is real through ways of behavior, but as an existing being he is concerned about himself, that is, about these relations and what is real.

Reality is of such a nature that everything real preempts man everywhere as effector and an effecting being, as a co-worker and something effected. Taken with an apparent historical indifference, the existentielle is not necessarily to be understood in a Christian way as with Kierkegaard, but with every respect to putting man to work as an effector of what is real. The echo which existential elements have found in the last decades is grounded in the essence of the reality which as will to power has made man into an instrument of making (production, effecting). This essence of Being can remain veiled in spite of Nietzsche, and even for Nietzsche himself. Hence the existentielle admits of manifold interpretations.

Its echo and predominance and the historically impossible pairing of Nietzsche and Kierkegaard are grounded in the fact that the existentielle is merely the intensification of the role of anthropology within metaphysics in its completion.

The manifold forms of the existentielle in poetry, in thinking, in action, in faith, in production. They can only be seen when the existentielle itself is experienced as the completion of the *animal rationale*. And this is possible only in the manner of the history of Being.

"World view" and the "existentielle."

"Metaphysics" and "anthropology."

Being as beingness and man as *animal rationale*.

The exposition of the narrowing down of the nature of existence starts with Schelling's distinction of "ground and existence."

To be shown:

1. How the usual distinction of *essentia* and *existentia* is hidden even behind this distinction.

2. Why this distinction gets formulated in peculiar versions which are even contrary to each other (for example, "Being and beings"; "existence and the existing being"; where "existence" now stands for "ground" and the existence mentioned before is formulated as the "existing being." This term is actually more accurate. It expresses the rank of realization and the producer, self-ensuring as effecting and will).

3. How Kierkegaard adopts this distinction by narrowing the concept of existence to the being a Christian of Christian existence. This should not be taken to mean that the nonexisting is the nonreal. If only man is the existing, precisely God is what is absolutely real and reality.

THREE

Recollection in Metaphysics

Recollection in the history of Being thinks history as the arrival, always remote, of the perdurance of truth's essence. Being occurs primally in this essence. Recollection helps the remembrance of the truth of Being by allowing the following to come to mind: The essence of truth is at the same time the truth of essence. Being and truth belong to each other just as they belong intertwining to a still concealed rootedness in the origin whose origination opening up remains that which comes.

That which is original occurs in advance of all that comes. Although hidden, it thus comes toward historic man as pure coming. It never perishes, it is never something past. Thus we also never find what is Original in the historical retrospect of what is past, but rather only in remembrance which thinks at the same time upon presencing Being (what has been in being), and upon the destined truth of Being. At times recollection in history can be the only viable way to what is primal for the mindfulness practiced by the perduring thinking of the history of Being.

Recollection in metaphysics as a necessary epoch of the history of Being gives us food for thought: that and how Being determines the truth of beings in each case; that and how Being opens out a realm of projection for the explanation of beings in terms of this determination; that and how such a determination first attunes thinking to the claim of Being, and compels a thinker to speak of Being in virtue of this attunement.

Recollection of the history of Being in metaphysics is a bestowal which explicitly and uniquely gives the relation of Being and man to awareness to be pondered. It requires the courage for a response to the claim which either confronts the dignity of Being or else contents itself with beings. Recollection of the history of Being entrusts historical humanity with the task of becoming aware that *the essence of man is released to the truth of Being* before any human dependency on powers and forces, predestinations and tasks. Hence he remains left out of his essence for a long time, as one let into the *insurrection* of *production* within Being's realm of opening up in the sense of unconditional objectification. Being first lets powers arise, but also lets them sink into what is without essence, together with their impotence.

Recollection in the history of Being continually entrusts the essence of man to Being, not individual man, but man at home in his decisive character, in order that Being may tower in the openedness of its own dignity and have a home in beings cared for by man's nature. Only from human being, that is, from the manner in which man grants the word of response to the claim of Being, can a reflection of its dignity shine forth to Being. In the timespan when Being delivers primordiality to the Open, and lets the purity of its freedom in relation to itself, and thus consequently its independence, too, be known and preserved, Being needs the reflection of a radiance of its essence in truth.

This need is not the restlessness of a lack. It is the self-containedness of the wealth of the simple. As the simple, the Origin grants its decisiveness in a parting in which it approaches itself as what is granting, and thus allows pure needlessness to be once more in its own origination. This needlessness is itself a reflection of what is primal, taking place as the appropriation of truth.

At times Being needs human being, and yet it is never dependent upon existing humanity. Humanity does stand in relationship to Being, since it is historical and knows and preserves beings as such. But human being's claim upon Being itself is not always granted by Being as the gift through which mankind may have as its own the privilege of participating in the appropriation of the truth of Being. At such a time there sometimes arises from the claim of Being the attempt at a response in which mankind must sacrifice the individuals addressed who recollect Being, and thus think its history from the essential past.

Recollection does not report on past opinions and representations about Being. It also does not trace the relations of their influence nor tell about standpoints within conceptual history. It is unconcerned with the progression and regression of a series of problems in themselves, which are supposed to constitute a history of problems.

Because we only know, and only want to know, history in the context of historiography which explores and exposes elements of the past for the purpose of using them for the present, recollection in the history of Being also falls prey to the illusion that makes it appear to be conceptual historiography, and a one-sided and sporadic one at that.

But when recollection of the history of Being names thinkers and pursues their thoughts, this thinking is the listening response which belongs to the claim of Being, as determination attuned by the voice of that claim. The thinking of thinkers is neither something going on in "heads" nor is it the product of such heads. One can always consider thought historiographically in accordance with such viewpoints, and appeal to the correctness of this consideration. However, one does not thus think thinking as the thinking of Being. Recollection of the history of Being returns to the claim of the soundless voice of Being and to the manner of its attuning. Thinkers are not reciprocally measured with regard to their accomplishments which deliver success for the progress of knowledge.

Every thinker oversteps the inner limit of every thinker. But such overstepping is not "knowing it all," since it only consists in holding the thinker in the direct claim of Being, thus remaining within his limitation. This limitation consists in the fact that the thinker can never himself say what is most of all his own. It must remain unsaid, because what is sayable receives its determination from what is not sayable. What is most of all the thinker's own, however, is not his possession, but rather belongs to Being whose transmission thinking receives in its projects. But these projects only bear witness to the dwelling[1] in what is transmitted.

The historicity of a thinker (how he is claimed by Being for history and co-responds to this claim) is never measured by the historiographically calculable role which his opinions, always and of necessity misunderstood in his own time, play in their public circulation. The historicity of a thinker, which is not a matter of him but of Being, has its measure in the original loyalty of the thinker to his inner limitation. *Not* to know this inner limitation, not to know it thanks to the nearness of what is unsaid and unsayable, is the hidden gift of Being to the rare thinkers who are called to the path of thought. On the other hand, historiographical calculation looks for the inner limitation of a thinker in the fact that he is not yet informed about things foreign to him which other and later thinkers accept as truth, sometimes only through his mediation.

We are not speaking here of the psychology of philosophers, but solely of the history of Being. However, the fact that Being determines the truth of beings and attunes a thinking to the uniqueness of a Saying of Being through the presencing of truth at times, and determines a thinker in his determinacy from such a determination, the fact that in all of this Being appropriates its own truth previously and always primally and that this is *the* appropriating wherein Being presences—this can never be proved from the perspective of beings. It is also inaccessible to every explanation. Being in its history can only be perdured in that perdurance which re-

---

1. *Befängnis.* A word which easily has negative connotations (of being caught, imprisoned, inhibited) in German. But Heidegger explained that he intends no such negative connotation, only the meaning of remaining within what is transmitted.

leases the structure of human being to the relation to Being for the sole primal dignity of Being, so that it may continually endure, standing in the preservation of Being.

What happens in the history of Being? We cannot ask in this manner, because there would then be an occurrence and something which occurs. But occurrence itself is the sole happening. Being alone is. What happens? Nothing happens if we are searching for something occurring in the occurrence. Nothing happens, *Appropriation appropriates.* Perduring the opening out, the origin takes the parting to itself. The appropriating origin is dignity as truth itself reaching into its departure. Dignity is what is noble which appropriates without needing effects. The noble of the worthy Appropriating of the origin is the unique release as Appropriation of freedom, which is unconcealment of concealment—because it belongs to the ground-less.

The history of Being, which is solely Being itself, casts only a dim light into the supposedly sole transparency of the certainty of completed metaphysical knowledge. However, metaphysics is the history of Being as the progression out of the Origin. This progression allows the return to become a need, and allows recollection in the Origin to become a needful necessity. That history of Being which is historically familiar as metaphysics has its essence in that a progression from the Origin occurs. In this progression Being releases itself to beingness and refuses the opening out of the Origin's originating. Beingness, starting as *idea*, begins the precedence of beings with regard to the essential character of truth whose essence itself belongs to Being. In that Being releases itself into beingness and withdraws its dignity in concealment, which is itself at the same time concealed, Being seems to leave the appearance of Being to beings.

Since man is singled out within beings because he knows beings *as* beings and, knowing them, is related to them without, however, ever being able to know, that is, to preserve as a consequence of this distinction the ground of that distinction, man struggles for manifold dominance in the area of beings left to themselves in the history of Being which is called metaphysics.

Beings are what is real. Reality rescues its essence in effecting, which brings the knowing will as its own essence to authoritative effectiveness. Reality transposes its essence to the multiple forms of the will. The will produces itself in the exclusiveness of its egotism as the will to power. But in the essence of power there is hidden the utmost abandonment of Being to beingness. Through this abandonment, beingness becomes machination. On the surface, machination appears in the form of the precedence of the actualization of what is planned and can be planned in the area of what is calculated as real. The precedence over Being of what is real as the only being is unconditional. Being appears only to be subjected to scorn each time. The name of this scorn is "abstraction."[2]

The precedence of what is real furthers the oblivion of Being. Through this precedence, the essential relation to Being which is to be sought in properly conceived thinking is buried. In being claimed by beings, man takes on the role of the authoritative being. As the relation to beings, that knowledge is adequate which is used up by reification in accordance with the essential manner of beings, in the sense of the real as calculable and ensured. Knowledge thus becomes calculation. The sign of the degradation of thinking is the elevation of logistics to the rank of true logic. Logistics is the calculable organization of the unconditional lack of knowledge about the essence of thinking, provided that thinking, essentially thought, is that projecting knowledge which unfolds in virtue of Being in the preservation of truth's essence.

The surrender in which Being abandons itself to the utmost deformation of essence of beingness (to "machination") is in a hidden way the self-suspension of the primal essence of Appropriation in the Origin which has not yet begun, not yet entered, its ground-

2. The meaning here is that the scornful attitude toward Being calls it an abstraction.

lessness. The progression of Being to beingness is that history of Being—called metaphysics—which remains just as essentially remote from the Origin in its start as in its finish. Thus metaphysics itself, too, that is, that thinking of Being which had to give itself the name "philosophy," can never bring the history of Being itself, that is, the Origin, to the light of its essence. The progression of Being to beingness is at the same time the primal refusal of an essential grounding of the truth of Being and the surrender in favor of beings of the precedence in the essential character of Being.

The progression from the Origin does not relinquish that Origin. Otherwise beingness would not be a mode of Being. The progression can also do nothing about the refusal of the Origin. The primal veils itself in this refusal to the point of insufficiency. But in the progression the distinction of Being and beings enters the truth (openness) of Being undetermined in its turn, without explicitly entering its grounded structure. However, the distinction of Being and beings rescues itself immediately in the form of that distinction which alone co-responds to the beginning of metaphysics because it receives its structure from beings and from the distinction of beings and Being.

Beings are. Their Being contains the truth that they are. The fact *that* beings are gives to beings the privilege of the unquestioned. From here the question arises as to *what* beings are. From the perspective of beings, whatness is thus the being first questioned. Here it becomes evident that Being determines itself only in the form of beingness and then through such determination itself only brings beings as such to presence. Only then is thatness explicitly distinguished from whatness *(idea)*. The distinction which becomes familiar under the name of the difference of *essentia* and *existentia* in metaphysics, but hardly becomes visible in its own transformations, is itself grounded in the primal and true distinction of Being and beings, which is not grounded and is at the same time hidden.

The primal distinction, however, is not an act which invades and coincides with what is factually undifferentiated of Being and beings. The distinction is primally rather the presencing of Being itself whose origination is Appropriation. The original distinction can never be reached by going back behind the distinction of *essentia* and *existentia*, which underlies all metaphysics and which has its core in the essential character of the *existentia*. On the other hand, the metaphysical distinction itself—that means always, the distinction which structures and underlies all metaphysics—must first be experienced in its Origin, so that metaphysics becomes decisive as occurrence of the history of Being, and relinquishes the illusory form of a doctrine and an opinion, that is, of something produced by man.

The history of Being is neither the history of man and of humanity, nor the history of the human relation to beings and to Being. The history of Being is Being itself, and only Being. However, since Being claims human being for grounding its truth in beings, man is drawn into the history of Being, but always only with regard to the manner in which he takes his essence from the relation of Being to himself and, in accordance with this relation, loses his essence, neglects it, gives it up, grounds it, or squanders it.

The fact that man belongs to the history of Being only in the scope of his essence which is determined by the claim of Being, and not with regard to his existence, actions, and accomplishments within beings, signifies a restriction unique in its manner. This restriction can become evident as a distinction as often as Being itself allows what takes place to be known if man may venture his essence which has sunk into oblivion for him through the precedence of beings.

In the history of Being, Appropriation makes itself known to humanity at first as a transformation of the essence of truth. This could give rise to the opinion that the essential character of Being might be dependent upon the dominance of the actual concept of truth which guides the manner of human representational thinking, and thus the thinking of Being. But the possibilities of the actual *concepts* of truth are delineated in advance by the manner of the *essence* of truth and the prevailing of this essence. Opening out is itself a fundamental characteristic of Being, and not only its consequence.

Recollection in the history of Being is a thinking ahead to the Origin, and belongs to Being itself. Appropriation grants the time from which history takes the granting of an epoch.[3] But that time span when Being gives itself to openness can never be found in historically calculated time or with its measures. The time span granted shows itself only to a reflection which is already able to glimpse the history of Being, even if this succeeds only in the form of an essential need which soundlessly and without consequences shakes everything true and real to the roots.

3. In a conference Heidegger amended the original *Zeit* (time) in the German text to read *Epoche* (epoch).

FOUR

Overcoming Metaphysics[1]

[The text contains notes on the overcoming of metaphysics from the years 1936 to 1946. Their major part was selected as a contribution to the Festschrift for Emil Pretorius; one section (XXVI) appeared in the Barlachheft of the state theater at Darmstadt 1951 (editor: Egon Vietta).

"Overcoming Metaphysics" from the volume *Vorträge und Aufsätze* was added to this book at the request of Martin Heidegger.]

I

What does "overcoming metaphysics" mean? In the thinking of the history of Being, this rubric is used only as an aid for that thinking to be comprehensible at all. In truth, this rubric is the occasion for a great deal of misunderstanding because it doesn't allow experience to reach the ground in virtue of which the history of Being first reveals its essence. This essence is the Appropriating

1. Although Heidegger uses the familiar word *Überwindung* for "overcoming," he means it in the sense of the less familiar word *Verwindung*. When something is overcome in the sense of being *überwunden*, it is defeated and left behind. This is not the sense Heidegger intends here. When something is overcome in the sense of being *verwunden*, it is, so to speak, incorporated. For example, when one "overcomes" a state of pain, one does not get rid of the pain. One has ceased to be preoccupied with it and has learned to live with it. Thus, to overcome metaphysics would mean to incorporate metaphysics, perhaps with the hope, but not with the certainty, of elevating it to a new reality.

in which Being itself is overcome. Above all, overcoming does not mean thrusting aside a discipline from the field of philosophical "education." "Metaphysics" is already thought as the destiny of the truth of beings, that is, of beingness, *as* a still hidden but distinctive Appropriating, namely the oblivion of Being.

Since overcoming is meant as a product of philosophy, the more adequate rubric might be: the past of metaphysics. Of course this calls forth new erroneous opinions. The past means here: to perish and enter what has been. In that metaphysics perishes, it *is* past. The past does not exclude, but rather includes, the fact that metaphysics is now for the first time beginning its unconditional rule in beings themselves, and rules as beings in the form, devoid of truth, of what is real and of objects. Experienced in virtue of the dawning of the origin, metaphysics is, however, at the same time past in the sense that it has entered its ending. The ending lasts longer than the previous history of metaphysics.

II

Metaphysics cannot be abolished like an opinion. One can by no means leave it behind as a doctrine no longer believed and represented.

The fact that man as *animal rationale*, here meant in the sense of the working being, must wander through the desert of the earth's desolation could be a sign that metaphysics occurs in virtue of Being, and the overcoming of metaphysics occurs as the incorporation of Being. For labor (cf. Ernst Junger, *Der Arbeiter*, 1932) is now reaching the metaphysical rank of the unconditional objectification of everything present which is active in the will to will.

If this is so, we may not presume to stand outside of metaphysics because we surmise the ending of metaphysics. For metaphysics overcome in this way does not disappear. It returns transformed, and remains in dominance as the continuing difference of Being and beings.

The decline of the truth of beings means: The openness of

beings and *only* beings loses the previous uniqueness of their authoritative claim.

III

The decline of the truth of beings occurs necessarily, and indeed as the completion of metaphysics.

The decline occurs through the collapse of the world characterized by metaphysics, and at the same time through the desolation of the earth stemming from metaphysics.

Collapse and desolation find their adequate occurrence in the fact that metaphysical man, the *animal rationale*, gets fixed as the laboring animal.

This rigidification confirms the most extreme blindness to the oblivion of Being. But man wills *himself* as the volunteer of the will to will, for which all truth becomes that error which it needs in order to be able to guarantee for itself the illusion that the will to will can will nothing other than empty nothingness, in the face of which it asserts itself without being able to know its own completed nullity.

Before Being can occur in its primal truth, Being as the will must be broken, the world must be forced to collapse and the earth must be driven to desolation, and man to mere labor. Only after this decline does the abrupt dwelling of the Origin take place for a long span of time. In the decline, everything, that is, beings in the whole of the truth of metaphysics, approaches its end.

The decline has already taken place. The consequences of this occurrence are the events of world history in this century. They are merely the course of what has already ended. Its course is ordered historico-technologically in the sense of the last stage of metaphysics. This order is the last arrangement of what has ended in the illusion of a reality whose effects work in an irresistible way, because they claim to be able to get along without an unconcealment of the *essence of Being*. They do this so decisively that they need suspect nothing of such an unconcealment.

The still hidden truth of Being is withheld from metaphysical humanity. The laboring animal is left to the giddy whirl of its products so that it may tear itself to pieces and annihilate itself in empty nothingness.

IV

How does metaphysics belong to man's nature? Metaphysically represented, man is constituted with faculties as a being among others. His essence constituted in such a way, his nature, the what and how of his Being, are in themselves metaphysical: *animal* (sensuousness) and *rationale* (nonsensuous). Thus confined to what is metaphysical, man is caught in the difference of beings and Being which he never experiences. The manner of human representation which is metaphysically characterized finds everywhere only the metaphysically constructed world. Metaphysics belongs to the nature of man. But what is this nature itself? What is metaphysics itself? Who is man himself within this natural metaphysics? Is he only an ego which first thoroughly fixates itself in its egoity through appealing to a thou in the I-thou relationship?

For Descartes the *ego cogito* is what is already represented and produced in all *cogitationes*, what is present without question, what is indubitable and always standing within knowledge, what is truly certain, what stands firm in advance of everything, namely as that which places everything in relation to *itself* and thus "over against" others.

To the object there belongs both the what-constituent of that which stands over against *(essentia-possibilitas)* and the actual standing of that which stands opposite *(existentia)*. The object is the unity of the constancy of what persists. In its standing, persistence is essentially related to the presentation of re-presentation as the guarantee of having-something-in-front-of-oneself. The original object is objectively itself. Original objectivity is the "I think," in the sense of the "I perceive" which already presents and has presented itself in advance for everything perceivable. It is the *subiectum*. In the order of the transcendental genesis of the object, the subject is the first object of ontological representation.

Ego cogito is *cogito: me cogitare.*

V

The modern form of ontology is transcendental philosophy which becomes epistemology.

How does such a thing arise in modern metaphysics? In that the beingness of beings is thought as presence *for* the guarantee of representation. Beingness is now objectivity. The question about objectivity, about the possibility of standing over against (namely, over against guaranteeing, calculating representation) is the question about knowability.

But this question is not really meant as the question about the psycho-physical mechanism of the procedure of knowing, but rather about the possibility of the presence of the object in and for knowledge.

"Epistemology" is viewing, *theoria*, in that the *on*, thought as object, is questioned with regard to objectivity and what makes objectivity possible *(he on)*.

How does Kant guarantee the metaphysical element of modern metaphysics through the transcendental manner of questioning? In that truth becomes certainty and thus the beingness *(ousia)* of beings changes to the objectivity of the *perceptio* and the *cogitatio* of consciousness, of knowledge; knowing and knowledge move to the foreground.

"Epistemology" and what goes under that name is at bottom metaphysics and ontology which is based on truth as the certainty of guaranteed representation.

On the other hand, the interpretation of "epistemology" as the explanation of "knowledge" and as the "theory" of the sciences errs, although this business of guaranteeing is only a consequence of the reinterpretation of Being as objectivity and representedness.

"Epistemology" is the title for the increasing, essential powerlessness of modern metaphysics to know its own essence and the ground of that essence. The talk about "metaphysics of knowledge" remains within the same misunderstanding. In truth, it is a matter of the metaphysics of the object, that is, of beings as object, of the object for a subject.

The mere reverse side of the empirical-positivistic misinterpretation of epistemology shows itself in the growing dominance of logistics.

VI

The completion of metaphysics begins with Hegel's metaphysics of absolute knowledge as the Spirit of will.

Why is this metaphysics only the beginning of the completion and not the completion itself? Hasn't unconditional certainty come to itself as absolute reality?

Is there still a possibility here of self-transcendence? Probably not. But the possibility of unconditional self-examination as the will of life is still not accomplished. The will has not yet appeared as the will to will in its reality which it has prepared. Hence metaphysics is not yet completed with the absolute metaphysics of the Spirit.

In spite of the superficial talk about the breakdown of Hegelian philosophy, one thing remains true: Only this philosophy determined reality in the nineteenth century, although not in the external form of a doctrine followed, but rather as metaphysics, as the dominance of beingness in the sense of certainty. The counter movements to this metaphysics belong *to* it. Ever since Hegel's death (1831), everything is merely a countermovement, not only in Germany, but also in Europe.

VII

It is characteristic for metaphysics that in it *existentia* is always consistently treated only briefly and as a matter of course, if it is treated at all. (Cf. the inadequate explanation of the postulates of reality in Kant's *Critique of Pure Reason.*) The sole exception is Aristotle, who thinks out *energeia,* without this thinking ever being able to become essential in its originality in the future. The transformation of *energeia* to *actualitas* and reality buried everything which became apparent in *energeia.* The connection between *ousia* and *energeia* becomes obscure. Hegel first thinks out *existentia,* but in his "Logic." Schelling thinks it in the distinction of ground and existence. However, this distinction is rooted in subjectivity.

A later and confused echo of Being as *physis* shows itself in the narrowing down of Being to "Nature."

Reason and freedom are contrasted with nature. Because nature is what-is, freedom and the ought are not thought as Being. The opposition of Being and the ought, Being and value, remains. Finally Being itself, too, becomes a mere "value" when the will enters its most extreme deformation of essence. Value is thought as a condition of the will.

VIII

Metaphysics is in all its forms and historical stages a unique, but perhaps necessary, fate of the West and the presupposition of its planetary dominance. The will of that planetary dominance is now in turn affecting the center of the West. Again, only a will meets the will from this center.

The development of the unconditional dominance of metaphysics is only at its start. This beginning starts when metaphysics affirms its deformation of essence which is adequate to it, and surrenders its essence to that deformation and fixates it there.

Metaphysics is a fate in the strict sense, which is the only sense intended here, that it lets mankind be suspended in the middle of beings as a fundamental trait of Western European history, *without* the Being of beings ever being able to be experienced and questioned and structured in its truth *as the twofoldness* of both in terms of metaphysics and through metaphysics.

This fate, which is to be thought in the manner of the history of Being, is, however, necessary, because Being itself can open out in its truth the difference of Being and beings preserved in itself only when the difference explicitly takes place. But how can it do this if beings have not first entered the most extreme oblivion of Being, and if at the same time Being has not taken over its unconditional dominance, metaphysically incomprehensible, as the will to will which asserts itself at first and uniquely through the sole precedence of beings (of what is objectively real) over Being?

Thus what can be distinguished in the difference in a way presents itself, and yet keeps itself hidden in a strange incomprehensibility. Hence the difference itself remains veiled. A sign of this is the metaphysico-technological reaction to pain which at the same time predetermines the interpretation of the essence of pain.

Together with the beginning of the completion of metaphysics, the preparation begins, unrecognized and essentially inaccessible to metaphysics, for a first appearance of the twofoldness of Being and beings. In this appearance the first resonance of the truth of Being still conceals itself, taking back into itself the precedence of Being with regard to its dominance.

IX

Overcoming metaphysics is thought in the manner of the history of Being. It is the preliminary sign of the primal incorporation of the oblivion of Being. More prior, although also more concealed than the preliminary sign, is what shows itself in that sign. This is Appropriation itself. What looks to the metaphysical way of thinking like the preliminary sign of something else, is taken into account only as the last mere illusion of a more primal opening out.

Overcoming is worthy of thought only when we think about incorporation. This perduring thinking still thinks at the same time about overcoming. Such remembrance experiences the unique Appropriating of the expropriating of beings, in which the need of the truth of Being, and thus the origination of truth, opens up and radiates upon human being in the manner of a parting. Overcoming is the delivering over of metaphysics to its truth.

At first the overcoming of metaphysics can only be represented in terms of metaphysics itself, so to speak, in the manner of a heightening of itself through itself. In this case the talk about the metaphysics of metaphysics, which is touched upon in the book *Kant and the Problem of Metaphysics,* is justified in that it attempts to interpret the Kantian idea from this perspective, which still stems from the mere critique of rationalist metaphysics. However, more is thus attributed to Kant's thinking than he himself was able to think within the limits of his philosophy.

The talk of overcoming metaphysics can also mean that "metaphysics" is the name for the Platonism portrayed in the modern world by the interpretation of Schopenhauer and Nietzsche. The reversal of Platonism, according to which for Nietzsche the sensuous becomes the true world and the suprasensuous becomes the untrue world, is thoroughly caught in metaphysics. This kind of overcoming of metaphysics, which Nietzsche has in mind in the spirit of nineteenth century positivism, is only the final entanglement in metaphysics, although in a higher form. It looks as if the "meta," the transcendence to the suprasensuous, were replaced by the persistence in the elemental world of sensuousness, whereas actually the oblivion of Being is only completed and the suprasensuous is let loose and furthered by the will to power.

X

Without being able to know it and without permitting a knowledge about it, the will to will wards off every destiny, whereby we understand by destiny the granting of an openness of the Being of beings. The will to will rigidifies everything in lack of destiny. The consequence of lack of destiny is the unhistorical. Its characteristic is the dominance of historiography. Historiography's being at a loss is historicism. If one wanted to construct the history of Being in accordance with the *historiographical* representational thinking common today, the dominance of the oblivion of Being's destiny would be confirmed by this mistake in the most blatant way. The epoch of completed metaphysics stands before its beginning.

The will to will forces the calculation and arrangement of everything for itself as the basic forms of appearance, only, however, for the unconditionally protractible guarantee of itself.

The basic form of appearance in which the will to will arranges and calculates itself in the unhistorical element of the world of completed metaphysics can be stringently called "technology." This name includes all the areas of beings which equip the whole of beings: objectified nature, the business of culture, manufactured politics, and the gloss of ideals overlying everything. Thus "technology" does not signify here the separate areas of the production and equipment of machines. The latter of course have a position of power, to be more closely defined, which is grounded in the precedence of matter as the supposedly elemental and primarily objective factor.

The name "technology" is understood here in such an essential way that its meaning coincides with the term "completed metaphysics." It contains the recollection of *techne*, which is a fundamental conditon of the essential developent of metaphysics in general. At the same time, the name makes it possible for the planetary factor of the completion of metaphysics and its dominance to be thought without reference to historiographically demonstrable changes in nations and continents.

XI

Nietzsche's metaphysics makes apparent the second to the last stage of the will's development of the beingness of beings as the will to will. The last stage's failure to appear is grounded in the predominance of "psychology," in the concept of power and force, in life-enthusiasm. For this reason this thinking lacks the strictness and carefulness of the concept and the peacefulness of historical reflection. Historiography rules and, thus, apologetics and polemics.

Why did Nietzsche's metaphysics lead to a scorn of thinking under the banner of "life"? Because no one realized how, according to Nietzsche's doctrine, the representational-calculative (empowering) guarantee of stability is just as essential for "life" as "increase" and escalation. Escalation itself has been taken only in the aspect of the intoxicating (psychologically), but not in the decisive aspect of at the same time giving to the guarantee of stability the true and ever new impulse and the justification for escalation. Hence it is the unconditional rule of calculating reason which belongs to the will to power, and not the fog and confusion of an opaque chaos of life. The misled Wagnerian cult imposed an artistic aura on Nietzsche's thinking and its presentation, which, after the process of the scorn of philosophy (that is, Hegel's and Schelling's) through Schopenhauer, and after Schopenhauer's superficial interpretation of Plato and Kant, prepared the last decades of the nineteenth century for an enthusiasm for which the superficial and foggy element of ahistoricality automatically serves as a characteristic of what is true.

Behind all this, however, lies the singular incapacity of thinking in terms of the being of metaphysics and recognizing the scope of truth's essential transformation and the historical sense of the awakening predominance of truth as certainty. Behind it, too, lies the incapacity of thinking Nietzsche's metaphysics in its relation to the simple paths of modern metaphysics in terms of this knowledge, instead of making a literary phenomenon out of it which rather overheats our brains than purifies, and makes us pause, and perhaps even frightens us. Finally, Nietzsche's passion for creators betrays the fact that he thinks of the genius and the geniuslike only in a modern way, and at the same time technologically from the viewpoint of accomplishment. The two constitutive "values" (truth and art) in the concept of the will to power are only circumscriptions for "technology," in the essential sense of a planning and calculating stabilization as accomplishment, and for the creating of the "creators" who bring a new stimulus to life over and above life as it is, and guarantee the business of culture.

All of this remains in the service of the will to power, but it also prevents the will to power's being from entering the clear light of the broad, essential knowing which can only have its origin in the thinking of the history of Being.

The being of the will to power can only be understood in terms of the will to will. The will to will, however, can only be experienced when metaphysics has already entered its transition.

XII

Nietzsche's metaphysics of the will to power is prefigured in the sentence: "The Greek knew and sensed the terrors and horrors of existence: In order to be able to live at all, he had to set up the radiant dream-creation of Olympus above them." (*Socrates and Greek Tragedy,* chapter 3, 1871. The original version of *Birth of Tragedy from the Spirit of Music,* Munich, 1933.)

The opposition of the "titanic" and the "barbaric," of the "wild" and the "impulsive" is put here on *one* side, and beautiful, sublime appearance on the *other.*

Although it is not yet clearly thought out and differentiated and seen from a unified perspective, the idea is prefigured here that the "will" needs *at the same time* the guarantee of stability and escalation. But the fact that will is will to power still remains concealed. Schopenhauer's doctrine of the will dominates Nietzsche's thinking at first. The preface to the work is written "on Schopenhauer's birthday."

With Nietzsche's metaphysics, philosophy is completed. That means: It has gone through the sphere of prefigured possibilities. Completed metaphysics, which is the ground for the planetary manner of thinking, gives the scaffolding for an order of the earth which will supposedly last for a long time. The order no longer needs philosophy because philosophy is already its foundation. But with the end of philosophy, thinking is not also at its end, but in transition to another beginning.

XIII

In the notes to the fourth part of *Thus spoke Zarathustra*, Nietzsche writes (1886): *"We are attempting a venture with truth!* Perhaps humanity will perish by it! So be it!" (WW XII, p. 307.)

An entry written at the time of *The Dawn of Day* (1880/81) reads: "What is new about our present position with regard to philosophy is the conviction which no age has ever yet had: *that we do not have the truth.* All men of earlier times "had the truth"—even the skeptics." (WW XI, p. 268.)

What does Nietzsche mean when he speaks now and then of "the truth"? Does he mean "what is true," and does he think this as what truly is, or as what is valid in all judgments, behavior, and life?

What does this mean: to attempt a venture with the truth? Does it mean: to bring the will to power into relation with the eternal recurrence of the same as what truly is?

Does this thinking ever get to the question as to *wherein* the *essential being* of truth consists and *whence* the truth of this *essential being* occurs?

XIV

How does objectivity come to have the character of constituting the essential being of beings as such?

One thinks "Being" as objectivity, and then tries to get to "what is in itself." But one only forgets to ask and to say what one means here by "what is" and by "in itself."

What "is" Being? May we inquire into "Being" as to *what* it *is?* Being remains unquestioned and a matter of course, and thus

96

unthought. It holds itself in a truth which has long since been forgotten and is without ground.

XV

There can be an object in the sense of ob-ject only where man becomes a subject, where the subject becomes the ego and the ego becomes the *ego cogito*, only where this *cogitare* is conceived in its essence as the "original synthetic unity of transcendental apperception," only where the apex for "logic" is attained (in truth as the certainty of the "I think"). Here the being of the object first reveals itself in its objectivity. Here it first becomes possible and, as a consequence, unavoidable to understand objectivity itself as "the new true object" and to think it unconditionally.

XVI

Subjectivity, object, and reflection belong together. Only when reflection as such is experienced, namely, as the supporting relation to beings, only then can Being be determined as objectivity.

The experience of reflection as this relation, however, presupposes that the relation to beings *is* experienced as *repraesentatio* in general: as re-presentation.

But this can become a matter of destiny only when the *idea* has become *perceptio*. The transformation of truth as correspondence to truth as certainty, in which the *adaequatio* remains preserved, underlies this change. Certainty as self-guaranteeing (willing-onself) is *iustititia* as the justification of the relation to beings and of their first cause, and thus of the belongingness to beings. *Iustificatio* in the sense of the Reformation and Nietzsche's concept of justice as truth are the same thing.

Essentially, *repraesentatio* is grounded in *reflexio*. For this reason, the being of objectivity as such first becomes evident where the being of thinking is recognized as explicitly brought about as "I think something," that is, as reflection.

XVII

Kant is on the way to thinking the being of reflection in the transcendental, that is, in the ontological sense. This occurs in the form of a hardly noticeable side remark in the *Critique of Pure Reason* under the title "On the Amphiboly of the Concepts of Reflection." The section is a supplement, but it is filled with essential insight and critical dialogue with Leibniz, and thus with all previous metaphysics, as Kant himself sees it and as it is grounded in its ontological constitution in egoity.

XVIII

Regarded from the outside, it looks as if egoity were only the retroactive generalization and abstraction of what is egolike from the individual "egos" of man. Descartes above all obviously thinks of his own "ego" as the individual person *(res cogitans* as *substantia finita).* Kant, on the other hand, thinks "consciousness in general." But Descartes also already thinks his own individual ego in the light of egoity which, however, is not yet explicitly represented. This egoity already appears in the form of the *certum,* the certainty which is nothing other than the guaranteeing of what is represented for representational thinking. The hidden relation to egoity as the certainty of itself and of what is represented is already dominant. The individual ego can be experienced as such only in terms of this relation. The human ego as the individual self completing itself can only will itself in the light of the *relation* of the will to will, as yet unknown, *to* this ego. No ego is there "in itself," but rather is "in itself" always only as appearing "within itself," that is, as egoity. For this reason, egoity is also present where the individual ego by no means presses forward, where it rather retreats, and society and other communal forms rule. There, too, and precisely there, we find the pure dominance of "egoity" which must be thought meta-physically, and which has nothing to do with naively thought "solipsism."

Philosophy in the age of completed metaphysics is anthropology (cf. *Holzwege*, p. 91 f.). Whether or not one says "philosophical" anthropology makes no difference. In the meantime philosophy has become anthropology and in this way a prey to the derivatives of metaphysics, that is, of physics in the broadest sense, which includes the physics of life and man, biology and psychology. Having become anthropology, philosophy itself perishes of metaphysics.

XIX

The will to will presupposes as the condition of its possibility the guarantee of stability (truth) and the possibility of exaggerating drives (art). Accordingly, the will to will arranges even beings as Being. In the will to will, technology (guarantee of stability) and the unconditional lack of reflection ("experience") first come to dominance.

Technology as the highest form of rational consciousness, technologically interpreted, and the lack of reflection as the arranged powerlessness, opaque to itself, to attain a relation to what is worthy of question, belong together: they are the same thing.

We are presupposing that why this is so and how it came to this has been experienced and understood.

We only want to consider the fact that anthropology is not exhausted by the study of man and by the will to explain everything in terms of man as his expression. Even where nothing is studied, where rather decisions are sought, this occurs in such a manner that one kind of humanity is previously pitted against another, humanity is acknowledged as the original force, just as if it were the first and last element in all beings, and beings and their actual interpretation were only the consequence.

Thus the solely decisive question comes to predominance: To

what form does man belong? "Form" is thought here in an indefinite metaphysical way, that is, Platonically as what is and first determines all tradition and development, itself, however, remaining independent of this. This anticipatory acknowledgment of "man" leads to searching for Being first of all and only in man's environment, and to regarding man himself as human stability, as the actual *me on* to the *idea*.

XX

In that the will to power attains its most extreme, unconditional guarantee, it is the sole criterion that guarantees everything, and thus what is correct. The correctness of the will to will is the unconditional and complete guaranteeing of itself. What is in accordance with its will is correct and in order, because the will to will itself is the only order. In this self-guaranteeing of the will to will, the primal being of truth is lost. The correctness of the will to will is what is absolutely untrue. The correctness of the untrue has its own irresistibility in the scope of the will to will. But the correctness of the untrue which remains concealed *as such* is at the same time the most uncanny thing that can occur in the distortion of the being of truth. What is correct masters what is true and sets truth aside. The will to unconditional guaranteeing first causes ubiquitous uncertainty to appear.

XXI

The will is in itself already the accomplishment of striving as the realization of what is striven for. What is striven for is explicitly known and consciously posited in the concept, that is, as something represented in general. Consciousness belongs to the will. The will to will is the highest and unconditional consciousness of the calculating self-guaranteeing of calculation (cf. *The Will to Power*, no. 458).

Hence there belongs to it the ubiquitous, continual, unconditional investigation of means, grounds, hindrances, the miscalculating exchange and plotting of goals, deceptiveness and maneuvers, the inquisitorial, as a consequence of which the will to will is distrustful and devious toward itself, and thinks of nothing else than the guaranteeing of itself as power itself.

The aimlessness, indeed the essential aimlessness of the unconditional will to will, is the completion of the being of will which was incipient in Kant's concept of practical reason as pure will. Pure will wills itself, and as the will is Being. Viewed from the perspective of content, pure will and its law are thus formal. Pure will is the sole content for itself as form.

XXII

In virtue of the fact that the will is sometimes personified in individual "men of will," it looks as if the will to will were the radiation of these persons. The opinion arises that the human will is the origin of the will to will, whereas man is willed by the will to will without experiencing the essence of this willing.

In that man is what is thus willed and what is posited in the will to will, "the will" is also of necessity addressed in its essence and released as the instance of truth. The question is whether the individuals and communities are in virtue of this will, or whether they still deal and barter with this will or even against it without knowing that they are already outwitted by it. The uniqueness of Being shows itself in the will to will, too, which only admits one direction in which to will. The uniformity of the world of the will to will stems from this, a uniformity which is as far removed from the simplicity of what is original, as deformation of essence from essence, although the former belongs to the latter.

XXIII

Because the will to will absolutely denies every goal and only admits goals as means to outwit itself willfully and to make room for this game; because, however, the will to will nevertheless may not appear as the anarchy of catastrophes that it really is, if it wants to assert itself in beings; it still must legitimate itself. The will to will invents here the talk about "mission." Mission is not thought with regard to anything original and its preservation, but rather as the goal which is assigned from the standpoint of "fate," thus justifying the will to will.

XXIV

The struggle between those who are in power and those who want to come to power: On every side there is the struggle for power. Everywhere power itself is what is determinative. Through this struggle for power, the being of power is posited in the being of its unconditional dominance by both sides. At the same time, however, one thing is still covered up here: the fact that this struggle is in the service of power and is willed by it. Power has overpowered these struggles in advance. The will to will alone empowers these struggles. Power, however, overpowers various kinds of humanity in such a way that it expropriates from man the possibility of ever escaping from the oblivion of Being on such paths. This struggle is of necessity planetary and as such undecidable in its being because it has nothing to decide, since it remains excluded from all differentiation, from the difference (of Being from beings), and thus from truth. Through its own force it is driven out into what is without destiny: into the abandonment of Being.

XXV

The pain which must first be experienced and borne out to the end is the insight and the knowledge that lack of need is the highest and most hidden need which first necessitates in virtue of the most distant distance. Lack of need consists in believing that one has reality and what is real in one's grip and knows what truth is, without needing to know in what truth *presences*.

The essence of the history of Being of nihilism is the abandonment of Being in that in it there occurs the self-release of Being into machination. This release takes man into unconditional service. It is by no means a decline and something "negative" in any kind of sense.

Hence not just any kind of humanity is suited to bring about unconditional nihilism in a historical manner. Hence a struggle is even necessary about the decision as to which kind of humanity is capable of the unconditional completion of nihilism.

XXVI

The signs of the ultimate abandonment of Being are the cries about "ideas" and "values," the indiscriminate back and forth of the proclamation of "deeds," and the indispensability of "spirit." All of this is already hitched into the armament mechanism of the plan. The plan itself is determined by the vacuum of the abandonment of Being within which the consumption of beings for the manufacturing of technology, to which culture also belongs, is the only way out for man who is engrossed with still saving subjectivity in superhumanity. Subhumanity and superhumanity are the same thing. They belong together, just as the "below" of animality and the "above" of the *ratio* are indissolubly coupled in correspondence in the metaphysical *animal rationale.* Sub- and superhumanity are to be thought here metaphysically, not as moral value judgments.

The consumption of beings is as such and in its course determined by armament in the metaphysical sense, through which man makes himself the "master" of what is "elemental." The consumption includes the ordered use of beings which become the opportunity and the material for feats and their escalation. This use is employed for the utility of armaments. In that in the unconditionality of escalation and of self-guaranteeing armament runs out and in truth has aimlessness as its aim, the using is a using up.

The "world wars" and their character of "totality" are already a consequence of the abandonment of Being. They press toward a guarantee of the stability of a constant form of using things up. Man, who no longer conceals his character of being the most important raw material, is also drawn into this process. Man is the "most important raw material" because he remains the subject of all consumption. He does this in such a way that he lets his will be unconditionally equated with this process, and thus at the same time become the "object" of the abandonment of Being. The world wars are the antecedent form of the removal of the difference between war and peace. This removal is necessary since the "world" has become an unworld as a consequence of the abandonment of beings by Being's truth. For "world" in the sense of the history of Being (cf. *Being and Time*) means the nonobjective presencing of the truth of Being for man in that man is essentially delivered over to Being. In the age of the exclusive power of power, that is, of the unconditional pressing of beings toward being used up in consumption, the world has become an unworld in that Being does presence, but without really reigning. As what is real, beings are real. There are effects everywhere, and nowhere is there a worlding of the world and yet, although forgotten, there is still Being. Beyond war and peace, there is the mere erring of the consumption of beings in the plan's self-guaranteeing in terms of the vacuum of the abandonment of Being. Changed into their deformation of essence, "war" and "peace" are taken up into erring, and disappear into the mere course of the escalating manufacture of what can be manufactured, because they have become unrecognizable with regard to any distinction. The question of when there will be peace cannot be answered not because the duration of war is unfathomable, but rather because the question already asks about something which no longer exists, since war is no longer anything which could terminate in peace. War has become a distortion of the consumption of beings which is continued in peace. Contending with a long war is only the already outdated form in which what is new about the age of consumption is acknowledged. This long war in its length slowly eventuated not in a peace of the traditional kind, but rather in a condition in which warlike characteristics are no longer experienced as such at all and peaceful characteristics have become meaningless and without content. Erring knows no truth of Being. Instead, it develops the completely equipped plan and certainty of all plans whatsoever in every area. In the encompassment (circle) of areas, the particular realms of human equipment necessarily become "sectors"; the "sector" of poetry, the "sector" of culture are also only the areas, guaranteed according to plan, of actual "leadership" along with others. The moral outrage of those who do not yet know what is going on is often aimed at the arbitrariness and the claim to dominance of the "leaders"—the most fatal form of continual valuation. The leader is the source of anger who cannot escape the persecution of anger which they only appear to enact, since they are not the acting ones. One believes that the leaders had presumed everything of their own accord in the blind rage of a selfish egotism and arranged everything in accordance with their own will. In truth, however, they are the necessary consequence of the fact that beings have entered the way of erring in which the vacuum expands which requires a single order and guarantee of beings. Herein the necessity of "leadership," that is, the planning calculation of the guarantee of the whole of beings, is required. For this purpose such men must be organized and equipped who serve leadership. The "leaders" are the decisive suppliers who oversee all the sectors of the consumption of beings because they understand the whole of those sectors and thus master erring in its calculability. The manner of understanding is the ability to calculate which has totally released itself in advance into the demands of the constantly increasing guarantee of plans in the service of the nearest possibilities of plans. The adjustment of all possible strivings to the whole of planning and guaranteeing is called "instinct." The word here designates the "intellect" which transcends the limited understanding that only calculates in terms of what lies closest. Nothing which must go into the calculation of the miscalculating of individual "sectors" as a "factor" escapes the "intellectualism" of this intellect. Instinct is the superescalation to the unconditional miscalculation of everything. It corresponds to superhumanity. Since this miscalculation absolutely dominates the will, there does not seem to be anything more besides the will than the safety of the mere drive for calculation, for which calculation is above all the first calculative rule. Until now, "instinct" was supposed to be a prerogative of the animal which seeks and follows what is useful and harmful to it in its life sphere, and strives for nothing beyond that. The assurance of animal instinct corresponds to the blind entanglement in its sphere of use. The complete release of subhumanity corresponds to the conditionless empowering of superhumanity. The drive of animality and the *ratio* of humanity become identical.

The fact that instinct is required for superhumanity as a characteristic means that, understood metaphysically, subhumanity belongs to superhumanity, but in such a way that precisely the animal element is thoroughly subjugated in each of its forms to calculation and planning (health plans, breeding). Since man is the most important raw material, one can reckon with the fact that some day factories will be built for the artificial breeding of human material, based on present-day chemical research. The research of the chemist Kuhn, who was awarded the Goethe prize of the city of Frankfurt, already opens up the possibility of directing the breeding of male and female organisms according to plan and need. The way in which artificial insemination is handled corresponds with stark consistency to the way in which literature is handled in the sector of "culture". (Let us not flee because of antiquated prudery to distinctions that no longer exist. The need for human material underlies the same regulation of preparing for ordered mobilization as the need for entertaining books and poems, for whose production the poet is no more important than the bookbinder's apprentice, who helps bind the poems for the printer by, for example, bringing the covers for binding from the storage room.)

The consumption of all materials, including the raw material "man," for the unconditioned possibility of the production of everything is determined in a concealed way by the complete emptiness in which beings, the materials of what is real, are suspended. This emptiness has to be filled up. But since the emptiness of Being can never be filled up by the fullness of beings, especially when this emptiness can never be experienced as such, the only way to escape it is incessantly to arrange beings in the constant possibility of being ordered as the form of guaranteeing aimless activity. Viewed in this way, technology is the organization of a lack, since it is related to the emptiness of Being contrary to its knowledge. Everywhere where there are not enough beings—and it is increasingly everywhere and always not enough for the will to will escalating itself —technology has to jump in, create a substitute, and consume the raw materials. But in truth the "substitute" and the mass production of ersatz things is not a temporary device, but the only possible form in which the will to will, the "all-inclusive" guarantee of the planning of order, keeps itself going and can thus be "itself" as the "subject" of everything. The increase in the number of masses of human beings is done explicitly by plan so that the opportunity will never run out for claiming more "room to live" for the large masses whose size then again requires correspondingly higher masses of human beings for their arrangement. This circularity of consumption for the sake of consumption is the sole procedure which distinctively characterizes the history of a world which has become an unworld. "Leader natures" are those who allow themselves to be put in the service of this procedure as its directive organs on account of their assured instincts. They are the first employees within the course of business of the unconditional consumption of beings in the service of the guarantee of the vacuum of the abandonment of Being. This course of business of the consumption of beings in virtue of the unknowing defense against unexperienced Being excludes in advance the distinctions between nations and countries as still being essential determinative factors. Just as the distinction between war and peace has become untenable, the distinction between "national" and "international" has also collapsed. Whoever thinks in "a European way" today, no longer allows himself to be exposed to the reproach of being an "internationalist." But he is also no longer a nationalist, since he thinks no less about the well-being of the other nations than about his own.

Nor does the uniformity of the course of history of our present age consist in a supplementary assimilation of older political systems to the latest ones. Uniformity is not the consequence, but the ground of the warlike disputes of individual intendants of the decisive leadership within the consumption of beings for the sake of securing order. The uniformity of beings arising from the emptiness of the abandonment of Being, in which it is only a matter of the calculable security of its order which it subjugates to the will to will, also conditions everywhere in advance of all national differences the uniformity of leadership, for which all forms of government are only one instrument of leadership among others. Since reality consists in the uniformity of calculable reckoning, man, too, must enter monotonous uniformity in order to keep up with what is real. A man without a uni-form today already gives the impression of being something unreal which no longer belongs. Beings, which alone are admitted to the will to will, expand in a lack of differentiation which is only masked by a procedure and arrangement which stands under the "principle of production." This seems to have as a consequence an order of rank; whereas in truth it has as its determining ground the lack of rank, since the goal of production is everywhere only the uniform vacuity of the consumption of all work in the security of order. The lack of differentiation, which erupts glaringly from this principle, is by no means the same as the mere leveling down, which is only the disintegration of previous orders of rank. The lack of differentiation of total consumption arises from a "positive" refusal of an order of rank in accordance with the guardianship of the emptiness of all goal-positing. This lack of differentiation bears witness to the already guaranteed constancy of the unworld of the abandonment of Being. The earth appears as the unworld of erring. It is the erring star in the manner of the history of Being.

XXVII

Shepherds live invisibly and outside of the desert of the desolated earth, which is only supposed to be of use for the guarantee of the dominance of man whose effects are limited to judging whether something is important or unimportant for life. As the will to will, this life demands in advance that all knowledge move in the manner of guaranteeing calculation and valuation.

The unnoticeable law of the earth preserves the earth in the sufficiency of the emerging and perishing of all things in the allotted sphere of the possible which everything follows, and yet nothing knows. The birch tree never oversteps its possibility. The colony of bees dwells in its possibility. It is first the will which arranges itself everywhere in technology that devours the earth in the exhaustion and consumption and change of what is artificial. Technology drives the earth beyond the developed sphere of its possibility into such things which are no longer a possibility and are thus the impossible. The fact that technological plans and measures succeed a great deal in inventions and novelties, piling upon each other, by no means yields the proof that the conquests of technology even make the impossible possible.

The realism and moralism of chronicle history are the last steps of the completed identification of nature and spirit with the being of technology. Nature and spirit are objects of self-consciousness. The unconditional dominance of self-consciousness forces both in advance into a uniformity out of which there is metaphysically no escape.

It is one thing just to use the earth, another to receive the blessing of the earth and to become at home in the law of this reception in order to shepherd the mystery of Being and watch over the inviolability of the possible.

XXVIII

No mere action will change the world, because Being as effectiveness and effecting closes all beings off in the face of Appropriation. Even the immense suffering which surrounds the earth is unable to waken a transformation, because it is only experienced as suffering, as passive, and thus as the opposite state of action, and thus experienced together with action in the same realm of being of the will to will.

But the earth remains preserved in the inconspicuous law of the possible which it is. The will has forced the impossible as a goal upon the possible. Machination, which orders this compulsion and holds it in dominance, arises from the being of technology, the word here made equivalent to the concept of metaphysics completing itself. The unconditional uniformity of all kinds of humanity of the earth under the rule of the will to will makes clear the meaninglessness of human action which has been posited absolutely.

The desolation of the earth begins as a process which is willed, but not known in its being, and also not knowable at the time when the being of truth defines itself as certainty in which human representational thinking and producing first become sure of themselves. Hegel conceives this moment of the history of metaphysics as the moment in which absolute self-consciousness becomes the principle of thinking.

It almost seems as if the being of pain were cut off from man under the dominance of the will, similarly the being of joy. Can the extreme measure of suffering still bring a transformation here?

No transformation comes without an anticipatory escort. But how does an escort draw near unless Appropriation opens out which, calling, needing, envisions human being, that is, sees and in this seeing brings mortals to the path of thinking, poetizing building.